Periodical Acquisitions
and the Internet

Periodical Acquisitions and the Internet has been co-published simultaneously as *The Acquisitions Librarian*, Number 21 1999.

The Acquisitions Librarian Monographic "Separates"

Below is a list of "separates," which in serials librarianship means a special issue simultaneously published as a special journal issue or double-issue *and* as a "separate" hardbound monograph. (This is a format which we also call a "DocuSerial.")

"Separates" are published because specialized libraries or professionals may wish to purchase a specific thematic issue by itself in a format which can be separately cataloged and shelved, as opposed to purchasing the journal on an on-going basis. Faculty members may also more easily consider a "separate" for classroom adoption.

"Separates" are carefully classified separately with the major book jobbers so that the journal tie-in can be noted on new book order slips to avoid duplicate purchasing.

You may wish to visit Haworth's website at . . .

http://www.haworthpressinc.com

. . . to search our online catalog for complete tables of contents of these separates and related publications.

You may also call 1-800-HAWORTH (outside US/Canada: 607-722-5857), or Fax: 1-800-895-0582 (outside US/Canada: 607-771-0012), or e-mail at:

getinfo@haworthpressinc.com

Periodical Acquisitions and the Internet, edited by Nancy Slight-Gibney (No. 21, 1999). *Sheds light on the emerging trends in selection, acquisition, and access to electronic journals.*

Public Library Collection Development in the Information Age, edited by Annabel K. Stephens (No. 20, 1998). *"A first-rate collection of articles . . . This is an engaging and helpful work for anyone involved in developing public library collections."* (*Lyn Hopper, MLn, Director, Chestatee Regional Library, Dahlonega, Georgia*)

Fiction Acquisition/Fiction Management: Education and Training, edited by Georgine N. Olson (No. 19, 1998). *"It is about time that attention is given to the collection in public libraries. . . it is about time that public librarians be encouraged to treat recreational reading with the same respect that is paid to informational reading . . . Thank you to Georgine Olson for putting this volume together."* (*Regan Robinson, MLS, Editor and Publisher, Librarian Collection Letter*)

Acquisitions and Collection Development in the Humanities, edited by Irene Owens (No. 17/18, 1997). *"CAN EASILY BECOME A PERSONAL REFERENCE TOOL."* (*William D. Cunningham, PhD, Retired faculty, College of Library and Information Service, University of Maryland, College Park*)

Approval Plans: Issues and Innovations, edited by John H. Sandy (No. 16, 1996). *"This book is valuable for several reasons, the primary one being that librarians in one-person libraries need to know how approval plans work before they can try one for their particular library. . . An important addition to the professional literature."* (*The One-Person Library*)

Current Legal Issues in Publishing, edited by A. Bruce Strauch (No. 15, 1996). *"Provides valuable access to a great deal of information about the current state of copyright thinking."* (*Library Association Record*)

New Automation Technology for Acquisitions and Collection Development, edited by Rosann Bazirjian (No. 13/14, 1995). *"Rosann Bazirjian has gathered together 13 current practitioners who explore technology and automation in acquisitions and collection development. . . CONTAINS SOMETHING FOR EVERYONE."* (*Library Acquisitions: Practice and Theory*)

Management and Organization of the Acquisitions Department, edited by Twyla Racz and Rosina Tammany (No. 12, 1994). *"Brings together topics and librarians from across the country to discuss some basic challenges and changes facing our profession today."* (*Library Acquisitions: Practice and Theory*)

A. V. in Public and School Libraries: Selection and Policy Issues, edited by Margaret J. Hughes and Bill Katz (No. 11, 1994). *"Many points of view are brought forward for those who are creating new policy or procedural documents... Provide[s] firsthand experience as well as considerable background knowledge...."* (*Australian Library Review*)

Multicultural Acquisitions, edited by Karen Parrish and Bill Katz (No. 9/10, 1993). *"A stimulating overview of the U.S. multicultural librarianship scene."* (*The Library Assn. Reviews*)

Popular Culture and Acquisitions, edited by Allen Ellis (No. 8, 1993). *"A provocative penetrating set of chapters on the tricky topic of popular culture acquisitions... A valuable guidebook."* (*Journal of Popular Culture*)

Collection Assessment: A Look at the RLG Conspectus©, edited by Richard J. Wood and Katina Strauch (No. 7, 1992). *"A well-organized, thorough book... Provides the most realistic representations of what the Conspectus is and what its limitations are... Will take an important place in Conspectus literature."* (*Library Acquisitions: Practice & Theory*)

Evaluating Acquisitions and Collections Management, edited by Pamela S. Cenzer and Cynthia I. Gozzi (No. 6, 1991). *"With the current emphasis on evaluation and return on funding, the material is timely indeed!"* (*Library Acquisitions: Practice & Theory*)

Vendors and Library Acquisitions, edited by Bill Katz (No. 5, 1991). *"Should be required reading for all new acquisitions librarians and all library science students who plan a career in technical services. As a whole it is a very valuable resource."* (*Library Acquisitions: Practice & Theory*)

Operational Costs in Acquisitions, edited by James R. Coffey (No. 4, 1991). *"For anyone interested in embarking on a cost study of the acquisitions process this book will be worthwhile reading."* (*Library Acquisitions: Practice & Theory*)

Legal and Ethical Issues in Acquisitions, edited by Katina Strauch and A. Bruce Strauch (No. 3, 1990). *"This excellent compilation is recommended to both collection development/acquisition librarians and library administrators in academic libraries."* (*The Journal of Academic Librarianship*)

The Acquisitions Budget, edited by Bill Katz (No. 2, 1989). *"Practical advice and tips are offered throughout... Those new to acquisitions work, especially in academic libraries, will find the book useful background reading."* (*Library Association Record*)

Automated Acquisitions: Issues for the Present and Future, edited by Amy Dykeman (No. 1, 1989). *"This book should help librarians to learn from the experience of colleagues in choosing the system that best suits their local requirements... [It] will appeal to library managers as well as to library school faculty and students."* (*Library Association Record*)

Periodical Acquisitions and the Internet has been co-published simultaneously as *The Acquisitions Librarian*™, Number 21 1999.

© 1999 by The Haworth Press, Inc. All rights reserved. No part of this work may be reproduced or utilized in any form or by any means, electronic or mechanical, including photocopying, microfilm and recording, or by any information storage and retrieval system, without permission in writing from the publisher. Printed in the United States of America.

The development, preparation, and publication of this work has been undertaken with great care. However, the publisher, employees, editors, and agents of The Haworth Press and all imprints of The Haworth Press, Inc., including The Haworth Medical Press® and Pharmaceutical Products Press®, are not responsible for any errors contained herein or for consequences that may ensue from use of materials or information contained in this work. Opinions expressed by the author(s) are not necessarily those of The Haworth Press, Inc.

The Haworth Press, Inc., 10 Alice Street, Binghamton, NY 13904-1580 USA

Cover design by Thomas J. Mayshock Jr.

Library of Congress Cataloging-in-Publication Data

Periodical acquisitions and the Internet / Nancy Slight-Gibney, editor.
    p. cm.
    "Has been co-published simultaneously as The acquisitions librarian, no. 21, 1999."
    Includes bibliographical references and index.
    ISBN 0-7890-0677-4
    1. Acquisition of electronic journals–United States. 2. Research libraries–Acquisitions–United States. I. Slight-Gibney, Nancy. II. Acquisitions librarian.

Z692.E43P47 1998
025.2'832–dc21   98-32065
    CIP

Periodical Acquisitions and the Internet

Nancy Slight-Gibney
Editor

Periodical Acquisitions and the Internet has been co-published simultaneously as *The Acquisitions Librarian*, Number 21 1999.

The Haworth Press, Inc.
New York • London

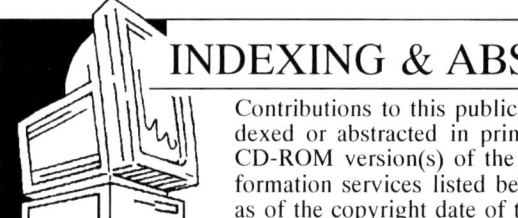

INDEXING & ABSTRACTING

Contributions to this publication are selectively indexed or abstracted in print, electronic, online, or CD-ROM version(s) of the reference tools and information services listed below. This list is current as of the copyright date of this publication. See the end of this section for additional notes.

- *Central Library & Documentation Bureau*
- *CNPIEC Reference Guide: Chinese National Directory of Foreign Periodicals*
- *Combined Health Information Database (CHID)*
- *Current Awareness Abstracts*
- *Educational Administration Abstracts (EAA)*
- *IBZ International Bibliography of Periodical Literature*
- *Index to Periodical Articles Related to Law*
- *Information Reports & Bibliographies*
- *Information Science Abstracts*
- *Informed Librarian, The*
- *INSPEC Information Services*
- *INTERNET ACCESS (& additional networks) Bulletin Board for Libraries ("BUBL"), coverage of information resources on INTERNET, JANET, and other networks*
- *Journal of Academic Librarianship: Guide to Professional Literature, The*
- *Library & Information Science Abstracts (LISA)*
- *Library and Information Science Annual (LISCA)*
- *Library Literature*
- *National Clearinghouse on Child Abuse & Neglect*
- *Newsletter of Library and Information Services*
- *NIAAA Alcohol and Alcohol Problems Science Database (ETOH)*
- *PASCAL, c/o Institute de L'Information Scientifique et Technique*
- *REHABDATA, National Rehabilitation Information Center (NARIC)*

(continued)

Special Bibliographic Notes related to special journal issues (separates) and indexing/abstracting

- indexing/abstracting services in this list will also cover material in any "separate" that is co-published simultaneously with Haworth's special thematic journal issue or DocuSerial. Indexing/abstracting usually covers material at the article/chapter level.

- monographic co-editions are intended for either non-subscribers or libraries which intend to purchase a second copy for their circulating collections.

- monographic co-editions are reported to all jobbers/wholesalers/approval plans. The source journal is listed as the "series" to assist the prevention of duplicate purchasing in the same manner utilized for books-in-series.

- to facilitate user/access services all indexing/abstracting services are encouraged to utilize the co-indexing entry note indicated at the bottom of the first page of each article/chapter/contribution.

- this is intended to assist a library user of any reference tool (whether print, electronic, online, or CD-ROM) to locate the monographic version if the library has purchased this version but not a subscription to the source journal.

- individual articles/chapters in any Haworth publication are also available through the Haworth Document Delivery Service (HDDS).

Periodical Acquisitions and the Internet

CONTENTS

Periodical Acquisitions and the Internet: An Introduction *Nancy Slight-Gibney*	1
Acquiring Electronic Journals *Kathryn D. Ellis*	5
Heads Up: Confronting the Selection and Access Issues of Electronic Journals *Faye A. Chadwell* *Sara Brownmiller*	21
Acquisition of Electronic Access to Information: More Money, More Records, More Time *Marjorie G. Wilhite*	37
Information Resources Development for Electronic Publications: An Academic Model *Patricia Promis* *Atifa Rawan*	51
Government Serials on the Internet: Challenges and Opportunities *Ted D. Smith*	71
A Survey of Standards for Identifying Serial Items on the Internet *Jennifer L. Marill*	83

The Internet: An Essential Tool for Law Library
   Serials Acquisitions   93
      Marla J. Schwartz
      Susan J. Kimball

Human Factors in the Electronic Technical Services   105
      Joni Gomez

Index   115

ABOUT THE EDITOR

Nancy Slight-Gibney, MA, MLIS, is Head of the Acquisition Department at the University of Oregon Library. She has nearly 20 years of experience in the field of library acquisitions. She received a Master of Arts degree in Anthropology from the University of Oregon and a Master of Library and Information Science degree from the University of Michigan.

Periodical Acquisitions and the Internet: An Introduction

Nancy Slight-Gibney

We are facing a profound change in scholarly communication. A digital scholarly information system has been evolving over the last decade and the potential for radically changing the way scholars, publishers and libraries function is remarkable. There are now thousands of journals available online, yet the distribution patterns are immature. In fact it is almost an oxymoron to describe the distribution as a pattern at all. It seems as if every electronic product is licensed, acquired, and made available in a unique way. Librarians struggle with the seemingly impossible task of creating procedures and workflows. In an address given at the ALCTS Business of Acquisitions Advanced Institute: Rethinking and Transforming Acquisitions, Clifford Lynch outlined the challenges that we face as we try to represent our institution's interests in the digital distribution system. First of all, there are few consensus answers; no "benchmarks" or "best practices" have emerged. Secondly, the acquisitions framework maps poorly into existing structures.[1] The linear model for the acquisition of print titles (collection development-acquisitions-vendor-publisher-acquisitions-cataloging-shelf-end user) is unsuited to the digital environment. Too much information needs to flow in too many directions. To the question of who or what unit in the library needs to be involved in the decision making, the answer seems to be: "Everybody!" At times it almost appears to be a three-ring circus. Those of us who have called publishers to clarify a point of price, licensing, or mode of access have found a three-ring circus at the other end too. In response to this complexity we are seeing the emergence of specialists in the acquisition of electronic resources.

[Haworth co-indexing entry note]: "Periodical Acquisitions and the Internet: An Introduction." Slight-Gibney, Nancy. Co-published simultaneously in *The Acquisitions Librarian* (The Haworth Press, Inc.) No. 21, 1999, pp. 1-4; and: *Periodical Acquisitions and the Internet* (ed: Nancy Slight-Gibney) The Haworth Press, Inc., 1999, pp. 1-4. Single or multiple copies of this article are available for a fee from The Haworth Document Delivery Service [1-800-342-9678, 9:00 a.m. - 5:00 p.m. (EST). E-mail address: getinfo@haworthpressinc.com].

© 1999 by The Haworth Press, Inc. All rights reserved.

Many acquisitions generalists, like myself, would like to believe that there is light at the end of the tunnel. We want to find ways to manage these business transactions and integrate them into the other work we do. Traditional subscription agents, not wanting to see their business diminish, also see themselves as having a role that is similar, but not identical, to their role in servicing print subscriptions. We now have the emergence of aggregators realizing the economies of scale, and information producers are recognizing the advantage in sales that aggregators can provide. Nevertheless, in spite of the similarities we see to the traditional publisher-distributor-library association, we must recognize that we are operating in a very different arena. We are leaving the world of purchasing a tangible item, where copyright law and fair use provisions guided us, and moving into the world of leasing access to data, where licensing and contract law make each resource unique.

The articles in this volume shed some light on the emerging trends in selection, acquisition, and access to electronic journals. Additionally there are discussions of the related issue of how the Internet has had a profound impact on even traditional acquisitions work. Standards for EDI (electronic data interchange) are examined that will continue to create improved efficiencies for the back room and more opportunities for customized delivery of information for the end user. These are fast moving targets that make any description almost obsolete before it gets into print, but the underlying approaches and problem solving strategies remain valid over time.

At the same time that we are beginning to see some answers to our current problems, we must realize that we are in the "early days of the emerging digital information system . . . just at the beginning of making broad, organizational change in the management of the archives of scholarship."[2] Libraries have been able to acquire a shrinking percentage of the scholarly output for years. Self-sufficiency was never really possible and successful systems of resource sharing developed. In the digital environment resource sharing takes on multiple new meanings as groups of libraries form consortia to pool their financial resources and provide their patrons with more information at less cost. Other groups of libraries are forming partnerships for archiving digital information. These cooperative arrangements create their own sets of challenges for acquisitions librarians in managing business transactions and evaluating service. Maintaining "control" of the process is not possible nor is it desirable. It is important for acquisitions librarians to stay focused on the fundamental mission and goals of the library and to develop knowledge and skills that will serve them and their institutions in the digital age. The electronic environment in which periodical acquisitions occurs requires that we:

- Understand the legal issues related to copyright law and contract law. A number of contributors to this volume refer to "Liblicense," a web site designed as a resource for librarians on issues related to licensing digital information.[3] An additional source is the Association of Research Library's web page, "Licensing Issues," which links to a number of sources on licensing and copyright.[4]
- Understand the complexity of the business environment we are working in. Skills in negotiating with vendors and evaluating their performance should translate into the new environment and these skills will be valued. However, we must also realize that assessment of a vendor's service will involve asking some new questions, such as evaluating the speed and reliability of the Internet connection.
- Understand that decision making will rarely be a solo operation. Decisions related to the acquisition of digital resources, from what to buy to whom to buy it from, will be made by groups of people. Communication skills are paramount. Keeping the information flowing to the people who need it will be a critical challenge.
- Understand that keeping technical skills up to date will require constant training and retraining. This is true for all levels of staff in the organization. Continuous learning will be a requirement of every job.
- Understand that the most important role of managers will be change management. We all will have to develop personal strategies for thriving in an environment characterized by high levels of uncertainty, unpredictability, and ambiguity. Effective leaders must provide the vision to see ahead as much as possible, empathy and stress reduction as we move faster and faster toward an unknown future, and conflict resolution when necessary.
- Understand that the strength of acquisitions librarians, indeed as it should be for all librarians, is in our ability to be both specialists and generalists. We constantly increase our knowledge and learn new details while not losing sight of the overview, and we can apply this perspective to solve problems in new situations.

Fundamental changes in scholarly communication are just beginning. Digital formats are mainly serving as substitutes or enhancements of print versions. In some cases the digital format is an incomplete version of the print. In the future, the traditional book or journal may cease to exist as the basic organizational framework for the production, distribution, and archiving of scholarship.[5] In the fully digital future, scholars may be their own publishers, with professional societies and research libraries taking on the distribution, access, and archiving roles. Yet in the only partly digital present, we live in two worlds. While we prepare ourselves to meet the challenges that the technology brings, we must not forget our essential role in connecting library patrons to the information they need, regardless of format. The articles in this volume illustrate that the Internet is both a tool for performing our traditional roles faster, better, cheaper (we hope), and a transforming technology that leads us into a future we can only begin to glimpse.

REFERENCES

1. Clifford Lynch, "How Electronic Content and Technology Are Changing the Business of Acquisitions" (paper presented at the ALCTS Advanced Business of Acquisitions Institute: Rethinking and Transforming Acquisitions, ALA Preconference, June 27, 1997, San Francisco, CA).

2. Joseph J. Branin and Mary Case, "Reforming Scholarly Publishing in the Sciences: A Librarian Perspective," *Notices of the American Mathematical Society*, 45, no. 4 (April 1998): 475-486.

3. Yale University Library, "Liblicense: Licensing Digital Information," <http://www.library.yale.edu/~llicense/index.shtml>.

4. Association of Research Libraries, "Licensing Issues," <http://www.arl.org/scomm/licensing/>.

5. Branin and Case, "Reforming Scholarly Publishing," p. 483.

Acquiring Electronic Journals

Kathryn D. Ellis

SUMMARY. Electronic journal acquisition is a complex and sometimes difficult process. This paper describes various decisions involved in acquiring electronic journals, addresses the nature of potential problems, and offers possible solutions. The discussion covers investigation and verification of electronic journal titles, complexities of ordering and receiving, and maintenance of ongoing availability of electronic journal titles. Rather than presenting step-by-step instructions, this paper encourages the reader to learn ways of looking at the situation and ways of understanding events, so the reader's decision-making becomes as well informed as possible. *[Article copies available for a fee from The Haworth Document Delivery Service: 1-800-342-9678. E-mail address: getinfo@haworthpressinc.com]*

INTRODUCTION

Electronic journals have existed for over two decades, but only in the last six years or so have their numbers exploded. Publishers and societies are beginning to see electronic journals as central to their missions rather than as experiments.[1] Libraries are purchasing more and more titles in electronic formats and find they must now incorporate electronic journals into their normal work rather than treating them as exceptions. Although electronic journals have become more common, they have not become significantly more standardized. In this respect they are very similar to print journals. This natural variety in electronic journals combined with the novelty of the medium makes them particularly challenging–for users and librarians alike.

Kathryn D. Ellis is Systems Librarian for Acquisitions and Processing, 308 Hodges Library, University of Tennessee, 1015 Volunteer Boulevard, Knoxville, TN 37996-1000.

[Haworth co-indexing entry note]: "Acquiring Electronic Journals." Ellis, Kathryn D. Co-published simultaneously in *The Acquisitions Librarian* (The Haworth Press, Inc.) No. 21, 1999, pp. 5-19; and: *Periodical Acquisitions and the Internet* (ed: Nancy Slight-Gibney) The Haworth Press, Inc., 1999, pp. 5-19. Single or multiple copies of this article are available for a fee from The Haworth Document Delivery Service [1-800-342-9678, 9:00 a.m. - 5:00 p.m. (EST). E-mail address: getinfo@haworthpressinc.com].

© 1999 by The Haworth Press, Inc. All rights reserved.

This paper focuses on acquiring and providing access to electronic journals. It presents alternatives which may be available at different stages in the process, warns of potential problems, and offers possible solutions. Although necessarily incomplete, it provides a starting place for those facing these decisions for the first time or for those looking for alternative procedures. Rather than presenting step-by-step instructions, this paper encourages learning ways of looking at the situation and ways of understanding events, so that decision-making becomes as well informed as possible.

Several major themes are presented here as issues to consider when acquiring electronic journals. The first is to know what the library is acquiring, who the users will be, and how the material will be used. The next involves the library's technical processes for placing orders and receiving materials. When acquiring electronic journals, some of these processes will resemble those used for other materials; others will differ. Ensuring ongoing availability of materials is the final theme. The issues presented here are not unique to electronic journals, but how libraries address them will usually be reconsidered for the new medium.

This discussion focuses on certain types of materials and steps in the acquisition process. It does not address collection development decisions. The assumption is that those responsible for selecting materials have already chosen electronic journal titles and that now the titles must be ordered, received, and made available for use. This paper considers only electronic journals for which an order must be placed, whether as an isolated subscription or in combination with other materials, print or electronic. Details of providing intellectual access to these materials and issues relating to free e-journals are beyond the scope of this paper. Finally, the opinions and suggestions in this paper are based on my own experiences and discussions with other librarians, publishers, and vendors and are not intended to dictate what is correct for any particular library.

FEATURES OF ELECTRONIC JOURNALS AND ELECTRONIC JOURNAL SERVICES

Although every electronic journal seems unique, nonetheless e-journals have common features which allow us to group them into categories. For one, electronic journals are either freely available or subscription based. This paper deals only with e-journals for which an order must be placed. Another distinction is the method of delivery, networked or not. Networked delivery mechanisms include online services and Internet applications, such as email and world wide web. In a 1996 article Duranceau et al. provide a useful distinction between what they call "first-generation" and "second-generation" network-based e-journals. Briefly, "first-generation" are older style e-journals, comprised mainly of ASCII text, delivered via email, while "second-generation" are newer style e-journals, consisting of formatted text including graphics and images, delivered via the world wide web.[2] Non-networked delivery mechanisms include CD-ROMs and diskettes. Journals distributed in this way either can be used on standalone workstations or can be networked by the library for its patrons. In this way non-networked delivery to the library can become networked delivery to the end user. Another possibility is for the library to load data from tape or ftp for networked use by patrons. This is an alternative form of networked delivery to the library, which then provides delivery to the end user. Some e-journals are available by only one method while others may have options from which to choose.

Electronic journals may be purchased by direct subscription, through a subscription vendor, or, in recent years, through a new type of aggregator service that provides access to collections of electronic journals as a group. These services open another subscription route to individual titles as well as to groups of titles and are themselves available either directly or through a vendor. Not every e-journal title is available by every method, though. Proper initial investigation of a title therefore includes determining the subscription options for that particular title. Furthermore, purchase options may sometimes influence the decision to buy a title or not.

The more recently developed electronic journal services offer functions unavailable in print. These e-journal services include many titles, sometimes focused on certain subject areas, sometimes extending across a broad range of subjects. The services allow users access to the full text of e-journals to which the library (or consortium) subscribes. Additionally, they often allow users to search across many or all titles in the service's database, regardless of whether the library subscribes to the titles or not. For articles retrieved through searching, users may usually view citations and/or abstracts, and some services enable users to order copies of articles to be sent directly to themselves, viewed online, or downloaded. Thus, these services blur the lines between ownership and access, subscription and document delivery, journal article and citation database.

Various organizations, including publishers, subscription agents, bibliographic utilities, and nonprofit organizations, have developed electronic journal services. Each developer takes a different approach to the role of the e-journal service and what it thinks libraries and publishers want from such services. Each hopes to consolidate electronic serials information and to provide an easier or more convenient way for patrons to use these titles, but does so with a different model.

The methods for subscribing to electronic journals through a service vary as well. Some service providers are serial vendors who fill orders for specific e-journal titles. Others handle no subscriptions to individual titles (the library is free to order from whomever it wants), but require the library to pay for an access account on the service. Some publishers provide access to their own titles and to titles of organizations with which they have agreements, regardless of how the library subscribes to the titles. Most electronic journal services have agreements with a limited, though sometimes large, set of publishers to provide access to their materials. Before a library decides to use a service, such a service must be fully investigated in its own right, in a manner similar to that in which an individual e-journal title is researched.

An upcoming development introduces yet another option for providing end-users access to electronic journal articles. Some citation database producers are developing ways to link directly from a citation in their database to the article itself. Libraries choose which e-journals to purchase and by what method they want to subscribe. Then, the citation database producer builds links where they exist. This new approach, in which a citation database can act as a front end to the library's selected e-journal collection, contrasts with that of electronic journal services that collect journals and provide search mechanisms to act like a citation database. This development represents another creative way to bridge the gap between users and the information they need and illustrates how libraries and librarians must continually adapt as new services develop.

INVESTIGATION AND VERIFICATION

Before ordering an electronic journal, it is important for the library to know what it is buying, who the users will be, and how the material will be used. These factors will probably be determined as collection development staff decide whether or not they want to purchase a particular title, and the acquisitions, serials, and systems staff will need to be informed as well. If this information is not communicated to acquisitions along with the order information, acquisitions staff should find the answers themselves before ordering. These factors have the potential to reverse an otherwise favorable decision to purchase a particular title, and it is usually better to check twice than to purchase something the library will not be able to use.

As this information is being gathered, one consideration is the position of the person answering the questions for the selling organization. A technical support person, rather than a sales person, may be more qualified to handle detailed, technical questions. For questions of legal terminology or conditions, counsel at both institutions may need to speak with each other, although a librarian should be involved, as well, if at all possible. As always, it is a good idea to have written confirmation of any answers which may be controversial or not obvious from other written sources, and it is important to consider whether the person giving the answer is able and authorized to provide that information.

One of the first points to consider is whether the library is buying access only and for what time period. The period of access may equal the subscription period, but that is not always the case. Some subscriptions include ongoing, future, "perpetual" access to material published during the subscription period, even if the subscription is later dropped. A related question is whether the library will "own" anything at the end of the subscription period. Access in perpetuity to the subscribed materials is a form of "ownership." Other items that could be owned include CD-ROM or diskette cumulations, downloaded copies, or even paper printouts. For e-journal subscriptions that come in combination with a print version, the library may, in the end, own only the print. Many electronic journals begin by offering free or inexpensive access during a trial period, typically ranging from a month to a year. These promotional offers can be an excellent way to practice with e-journals or to try out a new e-journal for the library. The price will usually go up at the end of the trial period, however, and the library will need to decide if the material fits into its collection guidelines and is worth the cost of subscribing.

Another task is to determine the technical requirements for the title in question. These requirements may include minimum versions of web browsers or helper applications, types of printers, amounts of disk space or computer memory, speeds of Internet connections, sizes and resolutions of monitors, etc. Is the library able to meet the requirements? If not at this time, what would the library have to do to meet the requirements, and are those steps in the library's plan? Many electronic resources have the advantage that users can access them from their homes, offices, or classrooms. If the library expects to provide remote access to this title, will users be able to meet the technical requirements? Will they need help to set up their computers for access, and is the library prepared to offer that help? If the library will not, where can users go for help? It may be necessary to work with the library systems staff, public services staff, and/or external computing services to find the answers to these questions and to devise a plan for providing e-journals to library users.

License agreements and other legal matters are also a major area to consider. Most electronic journal subscriptions require a signed license agreement of some sort. It is critical that the library understand the license agreement and its terms. It is also important to know who at the library or parent institution is legally authorized to sign license agreements and to verify a common understanding of all terms, such as "authorized user" and "site." If any question exists as to whether the institution can agree to its terms, the license should be reviewed by the institution's legal counsel. Librarians who know the meaning and service implications of the terms of the license should work closely with legal counsel. Counsel knows what is legal but has no way of knowing what is acceptable or reasonable from a library point of view. Counsel depends on librarians for that information. Negotiations, if any, will need to be conducted before the purchase can go forward. If both parties cannot agree on the terms of the license, then the purchase will not be possible. This situation does not arise often, but it has occurred. For more information on licensing and related issues see the web site *Liblicense: Licensing Digital Information* at http://www.library.yale.edu/~llicense/index.shtml (sic) or some of the articles mentioned in its bibliography.[3]

One last issue to investigate is what provisions have been made for archiving the electronic journal. Are they practical for the library and are there alternatives? If there are no plans yet, is the publisher willing to entertain suggestions from the library if the library wants to undertake an archiving project? The answers to these questions may not sway a decision to subscribe to an e-journal; however, it is well to learn the answers beforehand, so that everyone will know whether the content is expected to be available indefinitely or whether access to it could prove to be ephemeral.

COMPLEXITIES OF ORDERING

When it is time to order, acquisitions librarians will face another set of questions. As electronic journals become more common, and as librarians become more familiar with working with them, we will develop standardized ordering procedures. Until then, however, we need to address questions related to ordering e-journals on a title-by-title basis.

From whom should the library order this electronic journal? In general, e-journals are available at least one of three ways: direct from the publisher, through a subscription agent, or as part of an online e-journal service, such as Blackwell's Electronic Journal Navigator or OCLC's Electronic Collections Online. Some titles are available by all three routes, others by only one or two methods.

Given a choice between ordering direct and ordering from a subscription agent, most of the issues to consider are the same as for a print subscription–consolidation of orders and payment, timeliness of responses, customer service, and ease of communication, to name a few. One additional consideration for e-journals is whether the subscription source can provide the technical information the library needs. This is important during the verification process and will usually continue to be an issue throughout the life of the subscription. A vendor may not know the technical details of an e-journal as well as the publisher does. On the other hand, if the vendor supports the e-journal system and the publisher simply provides the data to go into the system, then the vendor may be more knowledgeable. It is possible in some cases to order through an agent but still communicate directly with the publisher for technical details. After the initial verification process, library staff will probably have a good idea of who knows what about this title.

To decide whether to order a title through an electronic journal service, if that is an option, will require collection development and acquisitions to work closely with each other. Traditionally, acquisitions determines from whom any particular item should be purchased. In the case of e-journal services, however, the means of acquisition and the information and services acquired are inextricably intertwined. The library must decide whether it wants the added value the service can provide, how the service will fit in with other titles and services offered by the library, and whether the price difference, if any, is justified by the additional functionality such a service offers. Questions of customer service, responsiveness, and business practice may be factors as well. Collection development and acquisitions will need to work together to determine the best outcome for the library as a whole.

Once the decision has been made to access a title through an electronic journal service, the order placement choices available to the library depend on the interaction among the particular title, the e-journal service selected, vendors the library uses, and whether the library is willing to order directly from the publisher. In many cases, an e-journal subscription will include both access and the journal content, but in some instances access and content may be separate. For example, if an e-journal service does not handle subscriptions to individual e-journal titles, then the library may need two separate orders, one for the title and one for access through the e-journal service. Theoretically, any of the three types of sources for e-journal subscriptions–e-journal services, subscription agents, and publishers–may offer either or both access and content to a particular title. Amid the many possibilities it is important to choose carefully what to order from whom and to understand the implications of that decision.

The next consideration is how well electronic journal subscription orders will coordinate with existing acquisitions practices. These orders need to be tracked, verified, and audited like orders for other library materials. The method of integrating e-journal orders with other orders depends in part on the degree of automation in the acquisitions process, which varies tremendously from library to library. Many e-journals can be ordered online. If both the library's and the seller's automation systems can handle electronic ordering, invoicing, and claiming, then the e-journal order may look very much like other orders processed electronically. If this is not possible for the library, then extra steps may be required to incorporate electronic journal orders into current processes. Of course, every library will have a unique set of technical processing issues to deal with when incorporating e-journal orders into the acquisitions work-flow.

VENDOR/PUBLISHER ONLINE SYSTEMS

As with print subscriptions, many electronic journals can be ordered from the seller through its own online ordering system. For some titles, this proprietary system must be used to place an order. For others one may choose between placing an order electronically or through more traditional means, such as postal mail, telephone, or fax. Even if a library decides to place orders by traditional means when possible, there may be situations in which online ordering is advantageous. Online ordering can be much faster and, therefore, especially appropriate for "rush" orders. It can be more accurate, because (we assume) there is no need for re-keying on the seller's end. In addition, ordering e-journals online can give library staff a chance to practice and experiment on a small scale with a new mode of ordering that is certain to increase in the future.

How knowledgeable library staff members are about online ordering depends on their experience, on the site they are ordering from, and on the help and training they receive from within the library. The ordering "address," whether an email, web, or postal address, will have been discovered in the selection/verification process. Knowing what to do with it is another matter. If the electronic journal is to be ordered via email, then library staff simply need to know the proper email address, what information to include and request from the seller, and how to use their local email system. If the seller's own online system is to be used, then library staff need to know how to access and use the system.

The issue of access raises several important questions–do library staff have the appropriate software? Is it configured properly? Do they know the usernames and passwords for the many different systems they may be asked to use? All these concerns must be addressed before staff can easily use these systems. Someone in the library needs to be a resource person for staff to contact when they need help or when something is not working properly. Some vendor/publisher systems are easy to use, with clear screen prompts and instructions. Others are less intuitive and staff may need significant training and help sheets. Slow response times from online systems and network congestion can lead to frustration on the part of staff who may feel it is inefficient to use such a system rather than ordering the "old" way. Good system design, accurate information, and consistent system responses go a long way towards improving staff views of a system.

Acquisitions staff are not the only ones in the library who may want to use vendor/publisher online systems. Many such systems contain more than just ordering information, and, because they contain information on a much larger body of material than that to which the library subscribes, they are valuable for information about items not in the library's collection. Collection development will find these systems useful for selection and verification work as well as for price information. Serials can use them to check the status of published issues when making claim decisions. In some cases, reference or interlibrary loan may be able to use them to help patrons with difficult citations.

As the number of vendor/publisher online systems used by library staff increases, so does the variety of access methods and passwords. Managing this information can pose a significant challenge. For each online system, staff need to know the preferred access method, username, and password. Some system passwords change on a regular basis. Some systems have multiple usernames and passwords corresponding to different functions or different levels of access. These passwords need to be kept secure, yet all staff in the library who need access need to know the passwords and access methods. This can be a particular challenge if access is managed in the acquisitions department but collection development functions, and therefore access needs, are distributed throughout the library.

ORDER INFORMATION

Whether using a vendor/publisher online system or not, the library and seller will need to work out, beforehand or through the first few orders, exactly what information each needs from the other and in what form. The seller will need certain information from the library to properly process the order. If email or other means are used, the library may need to make an effort to ensure all information is included. Similarly, the library needs certain information for paying invoices. The seller ought to supply this information, but until procedures are established the library should be vigilant to assure that everything is in order.

One can use many parallel modalities to order electronic journals. The telephone provides immediate feedback and is good for clarifying points of confusion. Email is convenient and fast, is independent of time zones, and provides a record (if temporary) of correspondence. Fax and postal mail still provide the most authoritative documentation. Expect that whatever means of communication the library employs will be used at some time or another for e-journal orders, sometimes all for the same order. Telephone, fax, email, postal mail, and web may well all be used before an order is complete and correct. This means flexibility and training are crucial. It can be helpful to remember that libraries, publishers, and vendors are all in the same situation as they try to figure out how to handle this new type of material.

An ordering challenge peculiar to electronic journals is the need to communicate technical information such as IP (Internet Protocol) numbers, domain names, or software types needed by the library. It is helpful to have a person in the library who can serve as technical contact for electronic journals. This person can be in acquisitions, serials, reference, collection development, or systems. She or he will have to work closely with people in all these departments as well as with publishers and vendors. Some information will be the same for many titles, other information will vary from title to title. Ideally the library contact person will manage all this information and gather new information as required.

"RECEIVING"?

Once an electronic journal has been ordered the acquisitions staff will want to verify that it is being "received" properly. What does that mean for an e-journal? Titles that come on a physical medium such as CD-ROM or floppy diskette can be checked-in the same way as paper journal issues. Similarly, first-generation e-journals are usually delivered to an email address, so those issues can be accounted for and gaps noted. This is not quite as convenient as postal mail delivery, however, because someone needs to check the email account for new issues on a regular basis. In some cases the only message is an announcement of available articles (like a table of contents). Nonetheless, the library is notified of what is published and when.

Defining "receiving" for second-generation electronic journals, which are not really "delivered" at all but simply made available to subscribers on the web, is more difficult. Accessing these e-journals is much more similar to using various online services than to using print journals. Journal volumes, issues, articles, parts of articles, and/or supplementary information are added to the web whenever the publisher/producer is ready. Typically, subscribers are not notified of such additions, so nothing prompts library staff to see whether an item is available. They must regularly check availability and rely on users to let them know of problems.

After a subscription has been ordered, the electronic journal provider must set up the library's access. This process can seem instantaneous, as in the case of an e-journal distributed by a listserv program, or it can take days or weeks. One detail to confirm when ordering is how the library will know that the order is complete and access available. Some e-journals will notify the library when access should be available. For other titles the library must test on a regular basis to see whether the e-journal is available and working properly.

Testing involves trying features of the electronic journal system from various types of equipment used in the library or on campus. Depending on the nature of the e-journal, features to be tested could include web or other access, searching, viewing full-text articles, printing, downloading, emailing results, etc. All important features should be tested from different machines, platforms, locations, and IP numbers as appropriate for users in the library and on campus. When someone finds a feature that does not work on a certain configuration, the library will need to decide how to handle that situation. It may be a problem that can be solved by working with the e-journal provider. Even if it cannot be solved, the library knows the problem exists and can advise users on alternative configurations or alternative features they can employ to achieve desired results.

PROVIDING ACCESS

At this point the library has verified receiving what it purchased with its subscription, but the library's users need to have access, both intellectual and physical, for the purchase to be worthwhile. How will users know this electronic journal exists and whether or not it will be helpful to them in their work? One possibility is to provide access to the resource through the library's catalog. Many catalogs now have the capability for including web addresses in records and displaying them as "live" links to the resource. Utilizing this feature of the catalog, when available, has the advantage of including the e-journal with its intellectual neighbors in the collection. Another possibility is to provide access through a library web page, along with other Internet resources pointed to by the library. These alternatives are not mutually exclusive.

Physical access to electronic journals is another issue. Is a title available through the library web site? Such access can enable the library to restrict access to authorized users. Is the title available only from certain machines in the library or on campus? If so, this seems to defeat the purpose of electronic communications, but if an e-journal requires special equipment or software or if it is restricted by license limitations, the library might choose to make it available in this way. Is the e-journal available to off-campus or dial-up users? The answers to these questions depend on the local infrastructure, especially authentication mechanisms; on the license agreement; and on the nature of the e-journal itself. These various factors interact in a complex manner, giving each electronic journal a unique combination of characteristics, with the result that every e-journal appears to be treated differently. Once again, managing this complexity is one of the major challenges inherent in maintaining electronic journal subscriptions.

ONGOING AVAILABILITY

As serialists know, journals change. In this respect, electronic journals are just like their paper predecessors, but, in addition to changes in frequency, publisher, and content, e-journals can also change Internet addresses, modes of access, helper applications, methods of printing, and even system features. As the product changes the library will have to adjust accordingly. Sometimes changes will provide more choices, other times they will reduce or eliminate choices altogether. Consequently, continuing to provide e-journal access to users in the most advantageous way becomes a major challenge.

After access has been established for a new electronic journal title and after initial testing of that title, the questions become whether the title is still available and how the library can tell if it is not. Regular testing should alert library staff to unavailability. While this testing need not be as comprehensive as the initial testing, it does need to be in-depth enough to determine whether the major features of the system still work for the library. How often this should be done depends on how stable the title seems and on staff work-loads.

Another, perhaps the major, way of finding out that an electronic journal is not working is for users to tell the library when they are having problems. In this case "users" may mean library patrons or other library staff. Of course, they need to know whom to contact when encountering problems, so the name or position of the responsible person should be listed wherever appropriate. Web pages can include an email link of some sort. A disadvantage of email links is that the contact person may receive questions she or he would rather not answer, such as reference queries or technical computer support questions that really have nothing to do with the resources listed on the page. An advantage is that all users can act as eyes and ears for the library, and the library finds out much sooner if something is broken or needs attention. Library staff and regular users can be especially helpful, if, knowing how the system should behave, they notice differences and let the contact person know.

The library can take several steps when a problem with an electronic journal is reported. First is to try to diagnose the problem on the library's end, making sure that all equipment is working properly and that the Internet address for the resource is current and correct. Once the library is fairly sure the problem is not on the library's end, then it should contact the e-journal provider and report the problem. The provider may or may not already be aware of the problem and may have an estimate of repair time. Sometimes it is something simple on the provider's end that they can fix right away. Other times it is more complex, and the provider needs time to diagnose and solve the problem. If they are not sure where the problem is, the library can try to work with them to locate the problem and help with its diagnosis and solution. If a long interruption in service is expected, the library should inform staff and users so they will not be frustrated trying to use a broken e-journal. If the resource is unavailable for a very long time, the library can consider negotiating for a credit, refund, or extended subscription period where appropriate.

The issues involved in managing an electronic journal collection are similar to those for managing access to vendor/publisher online systems within the library but more complex and on a larger scale. The intellectual and physical access considerations discussed earlier come into play here, because users need to know that the electronic journals exist and how to access them, including software requirements and Internet addresses. Users then need to be able to get into the e-journal system. Generally, they either must work from a computer in an Internet domain authorized to use the e-journal or must sign in with a username and password. If the library or campus has a good authentication system, authentication of users before they enter part of the library's web space and provision of "seamless" access to Internet resources from that point may be possible. Otherwise the library must find a secure method of communicating usernames and passwords to authorized users, including updates when they change–an especially difficult task when the user population is large and distributed, as in the case of a university. Finally, users need to know how to use the e-journal system. Some systems are self-explanatory or have online help while some include hard-copy documentation. Hard-copy documentation can be made available to library users and staff who want to look at it and for training purposes. The library can create additional online documentation and hold training sessions for interested users, depending on need, demand, and staff workloads.

OTHER ISSUES TO CONSIDER

Some other issues arise for the library when electronic journals are a part of the collection. Public service staff will need to know practical aspects of e-journal support, such as how users can print; whether helper applications are required to go with the e-journal; what kind of machines are capable of taking these modifications; whether users can email results or download results to diskette; and where diskettes are available if users do not have any. They should also have a sense of how intuitive the various e-journals are, especially for new or occasional users, and of what kind of help is available for users. Many of these questions can be addressed through handouts, signs, and training sessions, either in groups or one-on-one.

Training for electronic journals offers challenges not present in other forms of bibliographic instruction. In addition to teaching users about the kinds of information available in e-journals and how best to find them, library staff must address the variety of computer platforms, access methods, and printer setups patrons may encounter when using e-journals from various locations. For users of e-journals, each title (or group of titles with a common interface) is like a new system. Each system performs similar tasks in a slightly different way and uses different terminology. This situation is confusing to users, who are trying to figure out how to do a particular task. As users become more familiar with a variety of types of electronic journals they will need less help from library staff, but it will be a long time before many users enter a library knowing how to use e-journals.

Another consideration is whether or not articles from electronic journals can be "lent" through interlibrary loan (ILL). The first question is whether lending is allowed for a given title and, if so, under what conditions or rules. Some e-journals explicitly state whether ILL is or is not allowed and in what ways. Others make no mention of it, so the library must inquire. Some e-journals include ILL provisions in their license agreements while others do not. Here, communication within the library is very important. Usually acquisitions, serials, or collection development staff have been dealing with the e-journal subscription and know whether any provision for ILL has been made. They must communicate this information to ILL staff. Similarly, if ILL has requests for materials from an e-journal new to them, they should check whether such requests may be filled. This exemplifies the kind of information the technical contact person for electronic journals will likely have to manage.

Despite the potential problems associated with electronic journals, they hold certain advantages over print. A significant advantage is the ability to collect use statistics easily. Depending on system capabilities and how access is provided, use can be monitored locally or through the e-journal provider. Raw use information can then be compiled into usable statistics. It is important to understand exactly what is being measured. Hits on a web page, for example, do not necessarily mean visitors actually read what was on the page, and in some cases images on pages can skew the number of hits. Some monitoring programs record what domains access each resource, providing clues as to which groups of users benefit most from a particular resource. If there are limits on the number of simultaneous users, then programs should determine how often and how many people attempt to use the resource but are unable to, due to maximum allowable user load. Some systems even record how often sessions are allowed to sit idle until the system closes them rather than the user logging out when he or she is finished. All this information can help the library to plan for future services and to strategize about which resources to offer to whom and at what levels.

CONCLUSION

Electronic journals are here to stay, but they are not yet "taking over" nor are they standardized in any way. As a result, e-journals are not yet easy or straightforward for libraries to manage. Electronic journals promise many benefits, but also bear costs beyond subscription price. These costs include increased time needed to order and verify receipt of materials, legal costs, time and materials for staff and user training, monitoring of accessibility, and purchase and maintenance of printers, helper applications, and other peripherals.

User acceptance of electronic journals varies. Some users appreciate the added capabilities of searching and downloading or value the additional information available, such as supplementary materials, images, sounds, and hyperlinks. Library service improves in that material is always available for use, multiple simultaneous use is possible, and material cannot be stolen or mutilated by other users. On the other hand, electronic formats are not yet as convenient to read, mark up, and use as paper, and some users simply do not like them. Additionally, not all users have the equipment or skills (or time or desire to learn them) to take advantage of electronic journals. Some users prefer information in electronic format, some prefer paper, and some care only for the information itself, regardless of format. Perhaps the library's role includes not only helping patrons learn to use these new formats (even when they may not wish to) but also helping patrons learn how electronic formats fit into their overall information environment.

Journal titles already exist that are only available electronically and their numbers are increasing. If these titles are to be part of library collections, we must continue to develop methods of incorporating e-journals into our regular work and continue to look for ways to ease and expedite acquisition of these materials. Librarians, vendors, publishers, and users must all cooperate to establish how best to employ this new journal format for the benefit of all.

REFERENCES

1. Clifford Lynch, Keynote Address, presented at the 7th Annual North Carolina Serials Conference, Chapel Hill, North Carolina, 5-6 March 1998.

2. Ellen Duranceau, Margret Lippert, Marlene Manoff, and Carter Snowden, "Electronic Journals in the MIT Libraries: Report of the 1995 E-Journal Subgroup," *Serials Review*, 22, no. 1 (Spring 1996): 49-50.

3. *Liblicense: Licensing Digital Information* [http://www.library.yale.edu/~llicense/index.shtml] (April 1998). Liblicense (the web site and email list) are projects sponsored by Yale University, with Ann Okerson as Project Manager and Owner. Funding has been kindly provided by the Council on Library Resources, now called CLIR (Council on Library and Information Resources).

Heads Up:
Confronting the Selection and Access Issues of Electronic Journals

Faye A. Chadwell
Sara Brownmiller

SUMMARY. This article examines how collection development and acquisitions librarians can best adapt their policies and procedures to face the challenges of selecting and providing access to electronic journals. It emphasizes the necessary changes librarians should consider in their collection development policies, provides an overview of the benefits and disadvantages of electronic journals, and covers the extra dimensions that providing access add to selection decisions. It provides assistance to help librarians reap the most of the promise and potential of electronic journals. *[Article copies available for a fee from The Haworth Document Delivery Service: 1-800-342-9678. E-mail address: getinfo@haworthpressinc.com]*

INTRODUCTION

In her excellent overview of librarians' administrative angst surrounding electronic journals, Dana C. Rooks comments that "we as librarians must embrace the potential of electronic serials and adapt our resources to incorporate this new tool, as we have adopted microforms, online services, fax and

---

Faye A. Chadwell is Head, Collection Development at University of Oregon Library, Eugene, OR 97403-1299 (chadwelf@oregon.uoregon.edu). Sara Brownmiller is Systems Librarian at University of Oregon Library (snb@darkwing.uoregon.edu).

[Haworth co-indexing entry note]: "Heads Up: Confronting the Selection and Access Issues of Electronic Journals." Chadwell, Faye A., and Sara Brownmiller. Co-published simultaneously in *The Acquisitions Librarian* (The Haworth Press, Inc.) No. 21, 1999, pp. 21-35; and: *Periodical Acquisitions and the Internet* (ed: Nancy Slight-Gibney) The Haworth Press, Inc., 1999, pp. 21-35. Single or multiple copies of this article are available for a fee from The Haworth Document Delivery Service [1-800-342-9678, 9:00 a.m. - 5:00 p.m. (EST). E-mail address: getinfo@haworthpressinc.com].

© 1999 by The Haworth Press, Inc. All rights reserved.

other technologies" (p. 453).[1] Just how successful or wrought with failure have librarians been in their quest to "embrace the potential of electronic serials?" The truth is definitely in the telling and librarians' stories about handling electronic journals indicate varying levels of frustration and triumph. Consider these anecdotes, for example:

- A student user at a reference desk is thrilled that a journal is available electronically. She has a vision impairment ordinarily requiring that she pay someone to read an article to her. Because the electronic version is available and compatible, she can use specialized computer software in the library to have her computer read the materials to her.
- While working with a professor to obtain access to two electronic journals, librarians discover that the professor, as editor of one of the journals, does not even know that the publisher requires a licensing agreement. To top this, he also provides the incorrect URL for the other title he wants.
- A reference librarian easily resolves a user's dilemma when the user learns to her dismay that a necessary issue of a journal title has been sent from the library stacks to the bindery. Realizing that her library subscribes to the electronic version of this title, the savvy reference librarian immediately locates the desired issue on the library's web page.
- A collection development librarian admits to her colleagues that she avoids the difficulties of electronic journals by promptly shoving all flyers and notices about their availability into one of her desk drawers.

Certainly good evidence exists, especially beyond this last anecdote, to suggest that more and more libraries are accepting the challenge of providing access to electronic journals rather than shirking or hiding from the responsibility. An Association for Research Libraries' flyer detailing the results of a SPEC survey of ARL libraries suggested that as of 1994, 35 ARL libraries were receiving electronic journals. In her 1997 survey of 132 ARL academic and research libraries and three non-ARL academic libraries, Barbara Hall found that "The overwhelming majority of the responding libraries (91%) offer access to networked electronic journals. Of the 78 libraries providing access, almost all provide links to remote e-journal metasites or jumpstations (N.B. metasite is defined as a server providing both archives and Internet links across many disciplines, and jumpstation is defined as a Web page that has links to other sites but does not have stored archives)."[2]

Likewise there is sufficient evidence demonstrating that more and more publishers have begun publishing their titles on the Web. As of November 1997, three electronic journal aggregators, OCLC's FirstSearch Electronic Collections Online (ECO), Blackwell's E-Journal Navigator, and SwetsNet, could boast that they each will be providing full-text access for at least 500 to 1,000 electronic journal titles in the very near future.

Because of the rapidity of these developments, however, a high level of stress remains among librarians attempting to handle the changes electronic journals are bringing to libraries, especially in the collection development and acquisitions arenas. Some librarians would still choose to avoid facing the future. How best then to reduce the stress and ease the fears of librarians in the first place? That is, how can collection development and acquisitions librarians adapt their selection and acquisitions processes in order to make the best possible collection development decisions where electronic journals are concerned?

Collection Development Policy

For starters, collection development and acquisitions librarians need to adapt their collection development policies and procedures to address the specific demands of this format from the point of selection. Clear communication about collection development plans and decisions is crucial because of the wide impact even the selection of a single electronic journal title will have on multiple departments throughout a library. Successfully incorporating electronic journals will also mean understanding the considerable benefits of electronic journals and weighing these against their possible drawbacks when selecting a title or set of titles. In some cases, libraries may do well to switch from a print subscription to an electronic one; in other cases, the disadvantages may make a transition inopportune or even impossible for a particular library. Finally, collection development and acquisitions librarians must gain better comprehension of the many access issues that electronic journals present and/or librarians must collaborate with those individuals who have more experience with the provision of electronic access for library resources. Dealing with electronic journals offers librarians opportunities for collaborating with their colleagues that perhaps no other format has done.

To provide some common understanding of the issues involved in selecting and acquiring electronic journals, libraries might consider using a set of pre-order guidelines and providing these guidelines to everyone. The University of Oregon Library Systems developed such a set of guidelines which is a component of the Library's policy on electronic journals.[3] Even if some librarians only need to consult the form a few times, at least the guidelines will have served as an important education tool for learning more about the various issues. For others who may only need to consult the guidelines occasionally, they will always be readily available.

We have already noted that hundreds of electronic journal titles have become available in a rather short time frame. Librarians can assume that this number will only increase even as they celebrate adding their 2000th electronic journal to their collection. While the focus of many of these electronic journals remains in the sciences and in technical areas, coverage of the social sciences and the humanities is expanding daily. However, just because there is a growing and diverse array of available electronic journals from which to choose does not mean that librarians need to abandon the subject specific policies we have already established. First and foremost, when considering whether to subscribe to an electronic journal, collection development librarians should be sure that electronic journals meet the selection criteria in appropriate subject areas or disciplines already developed for formats such as print, videotapes, CD-ROMs, or microforms. As the University of Oregon Library System's collection development policy for electronic journals states: "Specifically their purchase should adhere to the chronological, geographical, language, and date of publication guidelines set forth in general and subject specific policies."[4]

The UO policy states further: "As with other material, subject specialists should also (1) consider future and present curriculum and research needs; (2) select materials which meet the standards the Library expects of all materials in regard to excellence, comprehensiveness, and authoritativeness, and; (3) weigh the purchase of a particular title against other possible acquisitions from the materials budget."[5] In more basic terms, if a library does not select books or printed periodicals in science and mathematics that focus on the nineteenth century and are published in a language such as Japanese or Tagalog, then it is highly unlikely that this library will focus its collection of electronic journals on subjects irrelevant to its defined user groups, their interests and needs, and the institutional mission. Since journal titles relate to the curriculum and research needs of a university or college or to specific patron needs in the public library arena, librarians also are not going to spend time and energy selecting free titles with no relevancy to library users. Focusing selection decisions on predetermined subject areas defined in collection development policies will not create new responsibilities for librarians.

Pricing Models

What is new with electronic journals is handling the various subscription options for electronic journals and their corresponding pricing models. These models are much more varied and complicated than just selecting between an individual and institutional subscription to a print title.

Here are some possible scenarios. First, libraries may obtain electronic access for free if they already subscribe to the print or when they place a subscription to the print version. On the other hand, if libraries have print holdings or seek to add a new title, they may obtain electronic access at generally 10 to 20 percent above the cost of the print subscription. If desired and feasible, they may obtain the information only in electronic format for a reduced price, usually 10 to 20 percent less than a print subscription would cost. In some cases, electronic access may cost as much as a print subscription. With some new titles, libraries will receive titles electronically because the publisher is issuing their new journal titles only in electronic format from the initial issue. Likewise, some publishers may opt to drop publishing the print version and move to only electronic availability from a certain point in time into the future.

Because many libraries are investigating the benefits of consortial purchasing, they should understand that consortial negotiations might complicate subscription options and pricing models immensely. Some publishers are quite consortium-friendly, while others do not want to deal with consortia or have yet to develop processes for handling consortia. Publishers may base consortial quotes on a number of criteria including the total number of subscriptions held among participants, the number of student FTE per participating institution, the amount of the materials budget per library, or some combination of factors.

In the past, publishers have offered package deals for buying a specified set of print titles. Whether considering print or electronic subscriptions, librarians will need to consider purchasing a bundle of titles that may include titles for which collection development librarians might not have previously elected to subscribe to in any format. These titles were simply outside the collecting scope of their libraries. Dealing in the electronic realm may increase the number of such package deals and libraries can expect to confront some publishers who only license access to their electronic journals if libraries subscribe to a pre-set package. Such bundling of titles will have less impact in a consortial setting, since there may be a broader variety of titles owned among consortial members than by a single institution.

Once a selection decision is made for an electronic journal, librarians must negotiate an acceptable licensing agreement before access is permitted. Collection development and acquisitions librarians have acquired some experience handling licensing agreements, and though more often the exception than the rule, even some printed serials titles have been subject to licensing agreements or leasing agreements. With electronic journals, handling licensing agreements is a given. Depending on a library's preparation and experience, this given is a necessary frustration or a frustrating necessity. Unfortunately (at least to date), licensing is not a part of the acquisition process of serials management that librarians can hand over to serials vendors. In fact, licensing electronic journals means that librarians must have more direct contact with publishers. Direct contact could initiate more positive interaction between serials publishers and collection development librarians. Without developing a completely separate article on licensing, librarians must consider how to provide for the broadest possible access to the greatest number of users. At the very least, librarians should not settle for fewer rights and more responsibilities in terms of copyright restrictions and provisions of access than they have experienced with printed materials. Important points to focus on when licensing a title include the number of users, restrictions on who has access, where users may gain access, how users may obtain access, and what users may do with the information in terms of downloading, copying, printing, and e-mailing.

Collection development librarians will probably always categorize their collections by the various subject areas to which they are attempting to provide coverage. But because librarians will probably deal directly with publishers when acquiring access to electronic journals, they must also begin to think about their journal collections in terms of the publishers who are providing access to the titles. At first, librarians may deem this shift in thinking an added frustration to handling electronic journals because they have to check the status of their print holdings publisher by publisher. We would emphasize again, however, that dealing more directly with publishers and accumulating knowledge of one's holdings by specific publishers will only increase librarians' understanding of individual publishers' subscriptions models and pricing practices. The benefits will be that collection development librarians improve their decision making about selecting journal titles, managing serials costs, canceling serials titles, and providing document delivery.

If a library is going to pay extra for electronic access (and since a library will definitely deal with hidden or indirect costs for providing access to some electronic journals), librarians do not want to expend their dwindling serials funds for electronic titles that represent no more than electronic copies of the print titles. Collection development librarians want to select titles that enhance or improve on what is available in print. They want to be sure that the promise of electronic journals pays off. To ensure this payoff, librarians must deliberate on an assortment of features specific to electronic journals, while they must weigh the format's advantages over print journals against its drawbacks. And of course, librarians must carry out this deliberation in addition to considering the standard collection development guidelines that cover language, chronological, or geographical focus.

SELECTION CRITERIA

Some of the features and corresponding issues to contemplate when selecting electronic journals include: number of users, increased access, supplemental information, updates, and added access to other titles, locating citations, articles, and journals, timeliness, searching and customization capabilities, adaptive technology, space issues, usage data, preservation and archiving, and site stability.

Number of users. Electronic journals should provide access to multiple users even if they are reading the same article or issue. Print journals limit access to one user per article, issue, or bound volume.

Increased access. Electronic journals should be available 24 hours a day outside the walls of libraries. With print journals, a user may want to read print journals at home, but most libraries will not allow journals to circulate outside the boundaries of their building, even sometimes limiting access just to sections of the building. A user has to photocopy the desired article(s) to take with her. Print journals are also not available when the Library is closed. Finally, print journals may disappear from their location on library shelves or be at the bindery. In these cases, they might be temporarily unavailable to users until they are reshelved or returned.

Supplemental information, updates, and added access to other titles. Because most libraries will seek access to electronic journals via the publisher or an aggregator, they should consider the possibility of supplemental information or added access. By supplemental information, we refer to electronic journals that provide links to supplementary materials, like that often found in an appendix. Librarians can liken updates to the content of electronic journals to newspaper publishers that provide various editions of their newspapers depending on the time of day when the issue is released. Added access to titles refers to when publishers provide access to the titles and abstracts to sets of journal issues–issues to which a library does not yet subscribe.

Locating citations, articles and journals. The advent of electronic journals and Web-based catalogs should make locating articles in journals much easier. More libraries, including the University of Oregon Library System, are cataloging electronic journals to which they subscribe and linking directly to them from their Web catalog. Simultaneously, many libraries are maintaining a website devoted specifically to electronic journals. Most librarians are familiar with the difficulties that novice library users face when trying to locate journals. More and more database aggregators and electronic journal aggregators provide direct access to full-text titles directly through an electronic index that is searchable via title, author or subject. Users may locate a citation or reference to an article in an electronic index and then link directly to the journal's content without ever having to check a library's catalog. Users should also be able to link to other relevant journals or to the footnotes and cited references through hyperlinks. With print journals, users had to locate the citation, check to see if their library owned the titles in the library's catalog, and then retrieve the necessary printed title from the stacks. If they located references to interesting or related articles, they had to plod through the same process again and again.

Timeliness. Electronic journals should be able to provide access to journal content in a more timely fashion than print journals. Often electronic journal publishers can provide access to content at least two to three weeks in advance of print. With print titles, libraries may often take at least two to three days after a title's arrival in order to make it shelf-ready.

Searching and customization capabilities. With journal information in electronic format, users should have greater searching and customization capabilities. Users must be able to search the table of contents from multiple issues, the full text of journal articles, as well as the title, author, and subject or topic covered. Publishers should also consider the possibility of allowing users to customize their use of electronic journals. For example, the Institute of Physics provides these personalization options: an individualized filing cabinet, a personalized main menu, an e-mail alerting service, and personalized default searches and configurable PostScript downloads. Users can search via the title, author, subject or topic covered for articles of interest in print journals or electronic indexes, but they do not have the capability of linking directly to the full text.

Adaptive technology. Used in conjunction with adaptive technology such as JAWS (Windows), ZoomText (Windows), Dragon Dictate (Windows), Outspoken (Mac), Inlarge (Mac), or Power Secretary (Mac), electronic journals should provide easier access to information for users with disabilities. Computerized readers allow visually challenged users to listen to desired materials that are available electronically so they do not have to depend on readers. Availability of journals at a terminal will also mean that users with disabilities do not have to wait for or schedule additional assistance with library staff to retrieve physical items from the stacks.

Space issues. In the future, electronic issues should largely eliminate space problems, although the Library will incur costs for properly archiving materials through its purchase and maintenance of appropriate software and hardware. However, as libraries have added journal titles and other print materials, they have gradually run out of physical space to house the title runs to which they subscribe. Not having to provide shelving space for long runs of journal titles means that libraries do not have to periodically seek funding for building expansions, compact shelving, or offsite storage.

Usage studies. Producers of electronic journals should be able to provide statistics on how a user consults a journal and how a user searched a journal electronically–by specific journal title or broad subject access. If usage studies are not possible, at the very least, librarians should consider devising some method of tracking how many times users consult a library's web page on electronic journals, if not specific titles. In these days of serious budgetary scrutiny and possible cancellation of titles, librarians need to assess how often library users are using journal titles. Planning and executing a usage study of print journals is labor and time intensive. Studying the usage patterns of print journals also may not accurately account for all types of internal uses.

Preservation and archiving. Libraries should have electronic access to the archives of electronic journals and they should have perpetual access to the information which they have purchased if they decide to no longer subscribe to a title. Despite the somewhat disheartening and low percentage of libraries participating in archiving, the outlook for (and so the promise of) archiving electronic journals remains positive. Publishers, such as Project Muse, are offering the annual cumulations of titles on CD-ROMs to subscribing libraries. Many publishers, especially societal publishers, are maintaining electronic access to their journal archives while electronic journal aggregators such as OCLC are willing to take on not only archiving responsibilities, but also perpetual access.

Site stability. Libraries should expect that the websites and URLs will remain relatively stable. If they change or disappear, publishers need to inform librarians so that they can make necessary changes to an individual library's Web pages or to links in Web catalogs. Librarians should also consider some mechanism for periodically checking websites using the available technology.

PROVIDING ACCESS

Knowledge or familiarity with technology eases the burden of selecting electronic journals. However, because electronic journals have varying degrees of access requirements, collection development and acquisitions librarians must also either learn the access lingo and gain the necessary skills or cozy up to someone who is more familiar with these issues.

To provide access to an electronic journal, librarians must be familiar with authentication methods used by the publisher to allow access, with the different electronic formats in which the journal may be available, and with the different Web applications and/or plug-ins which may be required to view the articles in an electronic journal. In addition to these, librarians must decide how to make their users aware of electronic journals, perhaps through the library's Web pages or through the library's catalog. The final access issue is perpetuity or archiving electronic information. Since the library is not physically acquiring an e-journal, how will the library be able to provide access when a subscription lapses or an electronic journal ceases publication?

Most electronic journals that a library subscribes to will be accessed remotely, with the contents of the journal residing on the computers of the publisher or vendor. Most publishers and/or vendors of electronic journals require that electronic access be limited to authorized users when access is available outside the library. Authorized users are usually defined as the primary constituency of an institution. For a university this would be the students, faculty and staff of the institution. For a public library, authorized users may be people with a valid library card.

Thus far publishers have allowed access to their publications by either requiring that a user come from an approved IP address, that the user enter an institutional login/password, or that the user establish her own account, usually coupled with IP detection. IP addresses are the physical addresses of a computer attached to the Internet and are usually seen in four parts: aaa.bbb.ccc.ddd. IP detection can be the easiest for users trying to connect to an electronic journal from a computer on campus–from an office or computer lab or dorm. The user simply has to know the URL of the e-journal or select the appropriate link from a Web page and the contents are delivered to them. IP detection, however, can be problematic when the publisher is unwilling to license an entire campus. For example, an entire university may be covered by a Class B domain, the first two segments of a computer's Internet address which could look like 129.334.xxx.xxx. Some publishers, however, restrict access to the Class C level, 129.334.295.xxx. For large institutions, the primary clientele of a physics journal, for example, may be served by more than a single Class C domain. With such a restriction placed by the publisher, some physics faculty and students may be denied access to this important material in their office or lab.

Reliance on IP address detection for access, however, presents serious problems for users who do not have remote access to the campus computing network. Thus one of the first issues to confront librarians setting up access to e-journals is how to verify that remote patrons are eligible users. On-campus patrons trying to connect to an electronic journal are usually not a problem because the IP address of the computer they are using falls within the approved range. However, one of the strengths of an electronic journal is its availability any time, anywhere. Some institutions are able to serve as the Internet Service Provider (ISP) for their authorized users, allowing students to dial into their campus computer network from home. When a student then ventures out onto the World Wide Web, her computer address is affiliated with her academic institution.

If the institution is unable to serve as the ISP for its students and faculty, does it have the means to authenticate students and faculty as being affiliated with an institution before a faculty member ventures out onto the Web? This is a critical issue confronting many libraries and colleges. Some vendors have programs that will do this, such as IAC's Remote Patron Authentication Service (RPAS). Innovative Interfaces Inc (III), although not an e-journal vendor, offers such a feature, Web Access Management, in their software, making it easier for III libraries to authenticate patrons for services other than their online catalog. There are also programs such as Kerberos, which allow host (IP) to host (IP) security by verifying that a user is eligible for services allowed to a specified range of IP addresses.

Rather than IP detection, some publishers of e-journals allow access to their publications by requiring the user to submit an ID and password. The use of IDs and passwords may not provide better security against unauthorized access to an electronic resource given the ease of electronic communication among friends and colleagues. IDs and passwords present their own problems to the library, specifically how the ID and password are distributed or shared among users who may legitimately access a specific publication. From a Web page, users can be instructed to contact the library for the required ID and password. Some libraries have created Web pages that provide password information, although the Web pages containing this confidential information are restricted to the institution's primary clientele. For some electronic publications, libraries may be able to write a script that logs a patron into a specific resource after confirming that the patron's IP address falls within permissible ranges. Publishers requiring use of an ID and password may also implement IP detection, looking first to see if a user comes from an authenticated IP address, then requiring the user to input an ID and password.

Another variation of the password method of access requires each user to register individually with the remote site. The patron provides information about her right to have access to an electronic journal, such as her institutional affiliation or a subscription number from an institutional subscription. The patron then creates a user ID and password for her own use. As patrons create an ID and password, they are usually required to acknowledge acceptance of copyright and appropriate use restrictions. Once this is done, the publisher allows access based solely on the user ID and password or may first utilize IP detection, followed by a registered ID and password. The use of individual IDs and passwords can help to reassure the publisher that each person accessing its service is aware of copyright and license restrictions about appropriate use of material obtained.

Once a library establishes access to an electronic journal, by providing appropriate IP addresses to the publisher or by implementing a publisher mandated password system, the librarians must be familiar with the formats in which a publisher will deliver the content of the electronic journals. Formats commonly in use today include proprietary formats like PDF (portable document format) requiring Adobe Acrobat or RealPage by Catchword to view the actual text, postscript files in various types of zipped or compressed formats, and text or Rich Text Format (RTF). Patrons new to the Web will need assistance to complete the setup of their own Web browser for full functionality or assistance using some of the helper applications on workstations within the library.

Proprietary formats, such as PDF, require the use of a helper application to display electronic articles. Articles in PDF or RealPage are basically an image of the actual text page. At present, this format may come the closest to delivering a version of the text, which in appearance looks like the original physical page. PDF documents require the patron to be able to access a helper application, Adobe Acrobat. Without Adobe Acrobat, the patron's Web browser will not be able to display the article. Articles from e-journals, which arrive at the patron's desktop as PDF documents, can be very large files. Network capacity available at an institution, both on and off-campus, may have a negative impact on the ability of patrons to easily and quickly retrieve articles from electronic journals.

In addition to PDF, many publishers and vendors offer access to their journals in a Postscript format. Postscript is a program developed by Adobe, which describes how a page should look to a Postscript-compatible printer, and produces a high quality look. Patrons must know how to download a Postscript file and to print in Postscript format to be able to read an article. E-journal articles in Postscript format, however, cannot be viewed before printing, unless an additional program, such as Ghostscript and Ghostview, resides on the workstation. Postscript files are frequently very large. Consequently, these files are usually compressed using a program such as gzip to speed transmission. The file must then be decompressed before it can be printed. Patrons will need to have access to the correct decompression program for their article.

Presently some electronic journals are available simply as text files, with basic HTML tagging to display them on the Web, providing only the text of the articles and not graphics or tabular data. The journals available from Project Muse at Johns Hopkins University Press are an example of articles available in this format. Even long articles can be quickly transmitted in this format. Another useful feature of articles in a text format is the ability to add hypertext links to the text of the article. Project Muse makes the footnote number in the article text a link to the footnote at the end of the article, while the footnote number in the footnote section returns the reader to the footnote within the article text. As more journals become available electronically, publishers will increasingly provide links to other electronic articles either from within the text of an article or from an article's bibliography.

Many helper applications, such as Adobe Acrobat, are freely available for downloading from the Web. However, librarians should determine in advance the specific requirements for each electronic journal. Does the text of the journal come in a proprietary format requiring the use of a specialized Web help application? Is this helper application easily and freely available? Is this helper application easy to install and use? Does the application allow the user to download the article for future use or printing? Newer versions of some

Web browsers automatically install many helper applications with the installation of the browser. However, libraries should keep in mind whether their workstations or their patrons' computers are sufficiently powerful to run the latest versions of both Web browsers and helper applications.

In addition to the access issues just discussed, libraries must decide how to alert their patrons to their ability to use electronic journals. Faculty and students are becoming increasingly aware of the gradual shift to electronic publishing. They may come to the library seeking access to publications they know to be available electronically. Many journal publishers offer their publications in multiple formats–print and electronic, with the electronic version available for no or little additional cost to libraries with current subscriptions to a print title. An increasing number of libraries are cataloging electronic journals, either by supplementing an existing serial record with the electronic information or by creating a serial record for the electronic version. Libraries with a Web interface for their online catalog can provide a hypertext link to an electronic journal allowing the patron to move easily from the online catalog to the electronic publication. With catalog records in place for electronic journals, patrons will look to the library for access to an electronic publication just as they have for print publications.

In addition to access through the online catalog, some libraries use their Web pages to alert patrons to the existence of electronic journals. This can be a simple alphabetical list or it may be a listing of titles by discipline. Updating Web pages can be faster than providing cataloging for electronic journal titles, especially when the cataloging of this new format must compete with the cataloging of traditional formats. However, libraries that maintain Web pages of their electronic journals will need to resolve when such a task is no longer necessary because electronic journals have become fully integrated into the collection.

ARCHIVING

The final issue for libraries to address, and the one that raises the most unanswered questions, is how to archive the information in electronic journals to insure that the information is available far into the future. With print publications, as long as the publications are produced with long-life, acid free paper, users can expect to get access to the information for perhaps one hundred years or longer. Not so with electronic information. The problem of archiving must actually be approached from two directions: first, from the technical side–will computers ten years from now be able to retrieve and display data created today–and from the policy side–who should have the responsibility to archive electronic information, the publisher or producer, the vendor who may or may not be the same as the producer, or the subscriber.

Librarians are certainly aware of these perplexing issues for archiving electronic information but a satisfactory solution has yet to be identified. From the technical perspective, what is the best medium for archiving electronic journal articles? Should it be on floppy disks, cd-rom, magnetic tape, or hard disk formats? Each medium has its advantages and disadvantages. Each of these can provide a short-term solution for archiving. Librarians should, however, be careful to adhere to current standards for existing technologies and plan to periodically reassess their archival choices to see that the stored data can be retrieved with existing technology. At what point will they need to reformat or refresh older data to insure its compatibility with the technology of the future?

Just as important as the technical access issues is who bears responsibility for this task. Librarians can immediately agree that electronic information needs to be preserved for future use. The difficult questions are who will do this and how. In the print world, publishers rarely possess archival responsibility, which has fallen to libraries to preserve and maintain information. Should this be the model for electronic journals as well? It certainly is not clear that libraries are taking on this responsibility. According to the same survey conducted by Barbara Hall, 75 percent of the responding libraries are not archiving electronic journals locally.[6] Most of those which do archive, archive "only a handful" which are typically "produced by the local organization."

Even if a publisher offers to archive and maintain its publications, the publishing world is very fluid. Publishers cease to exist or they merge with other publishers to form new entities who may not place any value on the archived collections. The complexity and cost of archiving electronic collections makes this a difficult but fundamental challenge for librarians.

The outlook need not be so bleak as Hall's statistics portend. Some libraries are investigating archival solutions through such collaborative efforts as the Committee on Institutional Cooperation's Electronic Journal Collection. (The CIC is an academic consortium of major research universities, mostly from the Big 10 Athletic Conference.) Another early solution to the archival issue is a commitment by some electronic journal aggregators, such as OCLC's FirstSearch Electronic Collections Online (ECO), to offer perpetual access to electronic information to the subscriber. The aggregator accepts the responsibility of monitoring and evaluating new technical developments and insuring that the electronic journal data can be retrieved with new technologies. Thus the electronic collections are archived once with access by many, rather than each library, or even a group of libraries, having to solve this problem individually. Only time will allow librarians to determine the feasibility of this alternative.

Despite the enormous changes since Dana Rooks' article in 1993, librarians should not expect our angst (or that of publishers and patrons) to magically dissipate. If we can predict anything with certainty, we should foretell that the angst would only be heightened. Likewise, electronic journals are not going to disappear during the course of most of our careers, no matter how many notices and advertisements we hide amidst a dated collection of conference badges. However, we can successfully maneuver through the maze of electronic journals if we adequately adapt our selection processes and procedures and if we address the specific demands of this format. Ironically, librarians may even find that dealing with the selection and acquisition issues of electronic journals may improve the ways in which they select and handle other formats, including print subscriptions. We can also accept that fluidity or flux will probably be the natural state for this format, although we might yearn for stability, consistency, and perpetuity and we might try to hide from the inevitability of change.

REFERENCES

1. Dana C. Rooks, "Electronic Serials: Administrative Angst or Answer," *Library Acquisitions: Practice & Theory*, 17 (1993): 449-454.

2. Barbara Hall, "From Archiving Electronic Journals: Current Practices and Policies in Academic Research Libraries, Summary of Presentation on Archiving the Internet by the ALCTS Computer Files Discussion Group, American Library Association Annual Conference," http://www-lib.usc.edu/Info/Acqui/research.html, June 28, 1997.

3. University of Oregon Libraries, "Collection Development Policy for Electronic Journals," http://darkwing.uoregon.edu/~chadwelf/ejoupoli.htm, August 20, 1996.

4. University of Oregon Libraries, August 20, 1996.

5. University of Oregon Libraries, August 20, 1996.

6. Hall, 1997.

Acquisition of Electronic Access to Information: More Money, More Records, More Time

Marjorie G. Wilhite

SUMMARY. Growth and change characterize the acquisition of electronic access to information as we currently know it. Budgets earmarked for electronic access increase year by year. Acquisitions staff endeavor to plan workflow and create records to track trial or free subscriptions as well as paid orders. It is important to retain record flexibility to accommodate changing order specifications and to provide useful management reports. The challenge of staying abreast of recent developments in the marketplace has increased as well. *[Article copies available for a fee from The Haworth Document Delivery Service: 1-800-342-9678. E-mail address: getinfo@haworthpressinc.com]*

The headline on a full page advertisement for 3M Innovation in the April 1997 issue of *American Libraries* announces, "The trouble with the Information Superhighway is there are no road maps, no marked exits, and too few drivers who know where they are going."[1] Some of the "too few" drivers are the collection management librarians, who year by year, are increasing their purchases of electronic access to sites on the highway. These acquisitions are accompanied by the responsibility for cataloging staff to accurately map the site descriptions and the responsibility for acquisitions staff to record the cost and all other details describing the pur-

---

Marjorie Wilhite is Team Leader for Serials Acquisitions, Central Technical Processing Services, University Libraries, The University of Iowa, 100 S. Madison, Iowa City, IA 52242-1420 (marjorie-wilhite@uiowa.edu).

[Haworth co-indexing entry note]: "Acquisition of Electronic Access to Information: More Money, More Records, More Time." Wilhite, Marjorie G. Co-published simultaneously in *The Acquisitions Librarian* (The Haworth Press, Inc.) No. 21, 1999, pp. 37-49; and: *Periodical Acquisitions and the Internet* (ed: Nancy Slight-Gibney) The Haworth Press, Inc., 1999, pp. 37-49. Single or multiple copies of this article are available for a fee from The Haworth Document Delivery Service [1-800-342-9678, 9:00 a.m. - 5:00 p.m. (EST). E-mail address: getinfo@haworthpressinc.com].

© 1999 by The Haworth Press, Inc. All rights reserved.

chase agreements required for electronic access. Acquisitions staff are the "travel agents." They make arrangements and pay for tickets which allow a single customer or multiple customers to travel . . . in vehicles which may change design at any minute . . . as the vehicles and passengers speed to sites which may alter their architecture . . . as the customers change their minds about where they want to go and what kind of vehicle they want to drive . . . all . . . right in the middle of the trip. Each ticket may allow permanent access to all portions of the site which were open during the life of the ticket. Or, upon ticket expiration, the tour group may be completely excluded until a new ticket is purchased. The purpose of this article is to explain the increased demands on serials acquisitions staff as they arrange for and then rearrange and alter the purchases of electronic access to information. It will cover licensing, a significant topic in itself, only by acknowledging that licenses are almost always required by the information package producers. Records prepared for the University of Iowa Serials Acquisitions Unit will serve as case study examples.

MORE MONEY

Access to electronic information requires additional budget allocations. Purchases of access to electronic information may be monitored nationally, regionally and locally. The Association of Research Libraries (ARL) compiles and publishes an annual volume, titled *ARL Statistics*, to describe the collections, staffing, expenditures, and public service activities for its more than 100 member libraries. A portion of these statistics are the numbers compiled by each institution to describe expenditures for current serials, number of current serials purchased, and current serials received but not purchased. It also includes statistics on the number of electronic databases available on institutional computers under the heading, "Collections–Computer Files." The instruction for completing question 10 which gathers the data on electronic products is, "Include the number of pieces of computer-readable disks, tapes, CD-ROMs, and similar machine-readable files comprising data or programs that are locally held as part of the library's collections available to library clients."[2] Thus, the number of physical items has been counted, but the current *ARL Statistics* volume assigns no expenditure amount to this portion of the information on Collections.

An *ARL Supplementary Statistics Questionnaire*, 1995-96, was submitted to institutional members. Question 5 was a request for expenditures on electronic serials. Question 5 instructions request the inclusion of, "Expenditures for serial publications whose primary format is electronic, e.g., paid subscriptions for electronic serials via the Internet, CD-ROM serials, licensing and/or purchasing of electronic serial publications (including indexes and abstracts).

Include only expenditures that are part of expenditures for Current Serials on line 17 of the ARL Statistics Questionnaire for 1995-96." The ARL is not yet publishing the dollar value spent for the electronic serials reported by its member institutions.

The final Budget Survey compiled by the Association for Library Collections and Technical Services/Collection Management and Development Section/Chief Collection Development Officers of Large Research Libraries Discussion Group does provide figures for the expense of purchasing electronic access. The allocation for electronic access has increased at a far greater rate than the average base budget increased. The report explains that in many cases electronic resources are acquired by the libraries with money outside a library's materials budget, such as the library's services budget, or completely outside of a library's total budget by state consortia or university computing centers. Only materials budget dollars are reported here. (See Figure 1.)

The University of Iowa Libraries have gathered information on the expense of acquiring electronic access to information since 1990/91. Figure 2 includes expenses for subscriptions because this dollar value does not include the expense of electronic access as contrasted to the records reported by the Association of Research Libraries. The two figures are combined in the report submitted to ARL.

MORE RECORDS AND MORE TIME

The challenge for acquisitions is to allocate more staff time to create additional and often more complex records and to track complex and chang-

FIGURE 1. Thirty-Nine Responses from the List of 46 Libraries in the Discussion Group Reported on Their Allocations for Electronic Resources for Fiscal 1996/1997. The Increase in the Average Allocation for Electronic Resources Exceeded the Average Base Budget Increase by 22.5% (1994/95), 15.4% (1995/96) and 15% (1996/97).

ALCTS/CMDS/Chief Collection Development Officers of Large Research LIbraries Discussion Group Final 1996/97 Budget Survey

Year	% Increase of Average Base Budget	Average Allocation– Electronic Resources	% Increase in Average Allocation–Electronic Resources
1993/94	5.3%	$261,707.00	
1994/95	5.5%	$334,007.00	28%
1995/96	3.6%	$397,086.00	19%
1996/97	6.0%	$479,163.00	21%

FIGURE 2. Chart Illustrating Materials Expense for the University of Iowa Libraries, Excluding the Law Library. Between 1990/91 and 1996/97 the Total Expense for all Materials Increased 30.9%, Paper Subscription Expense Increased 40.1% and Electronic Subscription Expense Increased 371.5%.

Fiscal Year	Total Cost for Materials	% Increase	Electronic Materials Costs	% Increase	Electronic/ Total Cost	Paper Subscription Costs	% Increase	Sub. Costs/ Total Costs
1990/91	4,233,753.99		92,375.91		2.2%	1,953,286.49		46.1%
1991/92	4,119,598.03	−2.7%	93,620.66	1.3%	2.3%	1,905,879.55	2.4%	46.3%
1992/93	4,386,064.55	6.5%	181,371.55	93.7%	4.1%	2,146,122.42	12.6%	48.9%
1993/94	4,550,969.67	3.8%	245,479.08	35.3%	5.4%	2,218,567.76	3.4%	48.7%
1994/95	4,807,771.58	5.6%	335,374.38	36.6%	7.0%	2,271,765.96	2.4%	47.3%
1995/96	5,204,237.69	8.2%	411,218.26	22.6%	7.9%	2,562,990.22	12.8%	49.2%
1996/97	5,543,183.32	6.5%	435,537.97	5.9%	7.9%	2,735,662.16	6.7%	49.4%

ing purchasing arrangements. The ALCTS/CMDS/Chief Collection Development Officers of Large Research Libraries Discussion Group's Report, 1996/97, includes an observation by Ann Okerson. She states, "I believe that when we ask how much is spent on electronic resources (or how many of them are part of the Library's collections/services, as ARL does), we could be asking the wrong question. Electronic resources are of many formats and sorts. The most important characterization for me is do we own or perpetually lease the resource, *or* do we merely access it. . . . It seems (to me) important that we make this distinction rather than the 'electronic' one in order to better understand the kinds of conceptual changes we are bringing about."[3] No statistics currently available from national groups express this distinction.

Because of the need to report more finely tuned statistics, not just on the number and costs, but also on the method of electronic access, it is worthwhile to devise a method to record each mode of access, the "vehicles," in a manner that can be read, sorted and compiled by a library management system. It is essential to separate the count and cost of electronic subscriptions from the subscriptions for paper format, even though the same title may be acquired in both.

The University of Iowa Libraries use the NOTIS system. It was implemented in 1988 and has been our first and only automated system. The NOTIS Order/Pay/Receipt records (OPRs) provide many fields which can be utilized by computer generated reports. In 1988 the L4 field with space for two characters was chosen for recording a code which translates into a count of subscriptions and continuations. (See Figure 3.)

```
ps = paid subscription          pc = paid continuation
gs = gift subscription          gc = gift continuation
es = exchange subscription      ec = exchange continuation
pm = paid membership
```

And now acquisition of various types of electronic access is also coded using the same field:

cd = electronic paid subscription, CD ROM format received more than once per year
cc = electronic paid continuation, CD ROM format received annually or less frequently
ts = electronic paid subscription, tape format, loaded locally
ws = electronic paid subscription accessed via the World Wide Web
wg = electronic gift subscription accessed via the World Wide Web
ln = OPR created to record LAN payments for electronic subscriptions

From the time of our first electronic purchase until March 1997 these orders were counted only as subscriptions or continuations just like serials in any other format. It may be wise to alter the new codes to make them express whether the purchase allows permanent retention of the information or is a lease arrangement.

Vehicles Used for Site Access

The University of Iowa Libraries currently have a choice of four models:

1. Single passenger, in CD ROM format. The product is issued with regular periodicity and mounted in a single access workstation. The contents may be leased or owned. The discs are checked in using the standard acquisitions workflow. The OPR's L4 field is coded "cc" or "cd" depending on the frequency of publication.
2. Multi-passenger, in CD ROM format. The single passenger CD ROM traveling space is expanded to accommodate more than one passenger by mounting it in a local LAN. The number of simultaneous users can be increased with limits imposed by the capacity of the server and the ability to meet the publisher's price and licensing requirements. The discs are paid for by the appropriate subject fund and the LAN access is paid for by a special fund earmarked for expanded electronic access. The dual funds make it desirable to create two order/pay/receipt records for each of these subscriptions, one for the CDs themselves and one to use for posting LAN payments. The LAN OPR's L4 field is coded "ln." Records for "ln" OPRs are not included in the count of subscriptions or continuations.
3. Multi-passenger in tape format. The tapes are handled in the normal acquisitions workflow and then mounted in the libraries' on-line system. The OPR's L4 field is coded "ts."
4. Multi-passenger using World Wide Web access. The publisher may set restrictions such as access only through registered IP numbers by a specified number of simultaneous users. The OPR's L4 field is coded "ws" or "wg."

As user interest and skill grow the current vehicle can be traded in for an improved model. For example, many institutional travelers can band together to negotiate the purchase or lease of a vehicle and access to a site. Any group of institutions with the legal right to form a purchasing consortia may work with a willing publisher. The University of Iowa is a member of the Committee for Institutional Cooperation, the CIC. A CIC position was established to manage negotiations for products desired by collection management in the member libraries, a clear indication of the large number of opportunities for purchase and the depth of interest in them. Other cooperative purchases have been arranged with our sister institution, Iowa State University.

FIGURE 3. A NOTIS Order.Pay.Receipt Record for a CD ROM Subscription. The L4 Field and Its Code "cd" are Underlined. The Code Is Used for System Generated Reports.

```
LTUL DONE                                          AEK3068
                                      NOTIS ACQUISITIONS           INJE
  UL SERIALS LC sn 93002394  ISSN 1068-1086 S/STAT c FREQ w S/T
  PatentImages <computer file>. US1991/001 (1 Jan. 1991)- -- New Haven, CT, USA :
    MicroPatent, 1991-
    PO : 004AEK3068  07/15/97 ORDUNIT: SA RECUNIT: SA SCOPE: 2
    VENDOR: MICROPATEN ACTINT: 0035 POP: x L1: us    L2:
    VA:
    NV:
    NO:
    SOURCE:  J Forys              REF: INFO;
    DIV 001 CCN 001 NOTE: ==1622
    SEND ALL DISCS--SUPER RUSH--ATTACH BLUE FLAG-GIVE TO ADD VOL  MED:    PCS:
    =>001 2Y CN |a engn,ref/1 |b Software;118 |v yr,no-no          ITEMS: 0
    001 BN 1991-              E        0.00 EN 00  MD 07/15/97 AD none
          FC ENGIN98   97/98 CUR usd AMT  0.00 CN 001 XPM a L3/4         cd
    002 R  1997:no.91-98 (1997:July 1-8)            MD 07/25/97 AD none
    003 R  1997:no.99-102 (1997:July 15)            MD 08/02/97 AD none
```

Shop until you drop! Are serials acquisitions staff the dropping shoppers? No, it must be the collection management staff. Today single access via a CD ROM is purchased. Tomorrow a local LAN with a specified number of simultaneous users seems to best fit the need. Day after tomorrow much expanded access through terminals with site registered IP numbers is judged to be the right bargain to serve the users. Negotiations on licensing terms and price consume enormous amounts of collection management time. The decisions to order, cancel, or upgrade are made by collection management staff. They are decisions which include details of negotiation that must be recorded. Bill Gates, in an article titled, "It's a Wired, Wired World" asks, "For example when a customer calls, does all the information about your dealings–the status of the account, any complaints, a history of who in your organization has worked with the customer–appear immediately on a screen?"[4] The good travel agent's record will include these details. By doing so there will be ready answers for patrons and library staff when it is time to arrange for a more modern mode of access. It will be possible to gather information for management reports needed to document prices for electronic access currently being purchased so that their costs can be compared and evaluated against new proposals offered by publishers and consortia.

Sites to Lease or Buy

Today serials acquisitions staff do not place nearly as many new orders for serials as they did in the 1960s and 1970s. Cancellations are more common. However, the evolution of electronic access has resulted in orders for some of the same titles in multiple formats. Examples are Project Muse and the American Institute of Physics journals. Multiple formats may be acquired simply because they exist for important serial titles. Researchers should be encouraged to experiment with electronic access. A test drive can tip the balance scale to favor the new model. Various arrangements for electronic access at the University of Iowa Libraries may be typical of experiences at other institutions.

Format Combinations

Project Muse. Project Muse initiated our first thoughts about the need for order aggregation. Johns Hopkins University Press had placed 40 of its journals online by February 1997 and had enlisted over 300 subscribers to the Project. In the fall of 1996 the Press announced they would give a 60% discount on the print journal title costs to Project Muse subscribers. The University of Iowa placed an order on January 23, 1997, after working with a trial subscription in late 1996. Subscriptions were already in place for the paper format of 39 of the 40 titles then assigned to Project Muse. Thirty of these subscriptions were distributed among three vendors. Would the vendors want to continue to handle subscriptions for which the publisher was awarding 60% discounts to Project Muse purchasers? We believed they would not, canceled the vendor orders and reordered the subscriptions for paper format for 1998 and the future directly with the publisher. The adjustment in record keeping required 30 cancellation letters, 30 new acquisition records for the subscriptions to paper format each cross referenced to the Project Muse order record and 30 new acquisition records for the electronic format. The acquisition records for electronic format are necessary if a count of Web accessed subscriptions is to be supplied by the library management system. (See Figures 4, 5, and 6.)

In 1997 the American Institute of Physics announced that all 16 of its journals are available through World Wide Web access at no additional cost to paper format subscribers. Not as many adjustments were needed to track this upgrade as for Project Muse because no additional charges were levied. An acquisition record was created for the electronic format of each title and cross referenced to the acquisition record for paper format with our standard "COMB" notation.

FIGURE 4. Project Muse Is Described by a Provisional Bibliographic Record Using 900 Tags. Each Subscription Title Is Listed in Alphabetic Order Following a 940 Tag. The NOTIS Record Number Is Included.

```
LTUL MORE                                              AHJ9535
                                      NOTIS CATALOGING        INCH
   UL FMT S RT a BL s T/C   DT 07/02/96 R/DT 07/12/97 STAT mm E/L 9 DCF    D/S S
   SRC ?  PLACE ???  LANG ???  MOD    OA ? REPRO    D/CODE ? DT/1 ???? DT/2 ????
   CONT ?    S/T    FREQ ? REG ? MED    GOVT ? ISDS ? CONF ? SLE ?


   924:10:  |a Project Muse.
   926:    :  |a Baltimore, MD :  |b Johns Hopkins University.
   940/1:   :  |a American imago.   >ADF8063
   940/2:   :  |a American Jewish history.   >ADF8644
   940/3:   :  |a American journal of mathematics.   >ADF9083
   940/4:   :  |a American journal of philology.   >ADH1521
   940/5:   :  |a American quarterly.   >ADG3732
   940/6:   :  |a Arethusa.   >ADF8789
   940/7:   :  |a Bulletin of the history of medicine.   >ADE6661
   940/8:   :  |a Callaloo.   >ADG3355
   940/9:   :  |a Configurations.   >AES0624
   940/10:  :  |a ELH.   >ADS3231
   940/11:  :  |a Diacritics.   >ADG9476
   940/12:  :  |a Eighteenth-century life.   >ADE4112
   940/13:  :  |a Eighteenth-century studies.   >ADH5345
   940/14:  :  |a The Henry James review.   >ADC8288
   940/15:  :  |a Imagine.   >ADE5339
   940/16:  :  |a Journal of democracy.   >AEL8139
   940/17:  :  |a Journal of early Christian studies.   >AEW4536
   940/18:  :  |a Journal of modern Greek studies.   >ADC0802
   940/19:  :  |a Journal of the history of ideas.   >ADN9190
   940/20:  :  |a Late imperial China.   >ADD7198
   940/21:  :  |a Literature and medicine.   >ADE4452
   940/22:  :  |a The lion and the unicorn.   >ADC5196
   940/23:  :  |a MLN.   >ADL7370
   940/24:  :  |a Milton quarterly.   >ADM1004
   940/25:  :  |a Modern fiction studies.   >ADM1566
   940/26:  :  |a Modern Judaism.   >ADD3437
   940/27:  :  |a Modernism/modernity.   >AGJ3838
   940/28:  :  |a New literary history.   >ADD3437
```

FIGURE 4 (continued)

```
940/29:   :  |a Performing arts journal.  >ADD3437
940/30:   :  |a Philosophy and literature.  >ADP1645
940/31:   :  |a Postmodern culture <computer file>  >AEE1519
940/32:   :  |a Prooftexts.  >ADD1273
940/33:   :  |a Review of higher education.  >ADP8928
940/34:   :  |a Reviews in American history.  >ADP8878
940/35:   :  |a SAIS review (Washington, D.C. : 1981)  >ADC4802
940/36:   :  |a Theatre journal.  >ADQ4959
940/37:   :  |a Theatre topics.  >AEH0095
940/38:   :  |a Wide angle.  >ADR0415
940/39:   :  |a World politics.  >ADR2092
940/40:   :  |a Yale journal of criticism.  >ADC3719
```

FIGURE 5. The Order/Pay/Receipt Record for the Paper Format of American Imago Is Linked to the Project Muse Order by Referring to a Combination Order (COMB AHJ9535).

```
LTUL DONE                                          ADF8063
                                NOTIS ACQUISITIONS        TLBA
    UL SERIALS ISSN 0065-860X S/STAT c FREQ q S/T p
    The American imago. v. 1-   Nov. 1939- -- Detroit <etc.> Wayne State University
       Press.
    PO : 002ADF8063  06/21/97  ORDUNIT: SA  RECUNIT: SA  SCOPE: 2
    VENDOR: JOHNSHOP   ACTINT: 0450  POP:   L1: us   L2:
    VA:


    NV: w;Sub. formerly handled by a Vendor;Now part of Project Muse = 60% discount
    NO: reorder;COMB (AHJ9535)
    SOURCE:                        REF: INFO;
    DIV 001 CCN 001 NOTE: ==1922==
                    REORDER - GIVE V.55:NO.1 (1998) to JW    MED:    PCS:
    =>001 2X CN |a main,per/1 |b none                        ITEMS: 42
    001 AC v.55 (1998)-        E       0.00 EN 00  MD 06/21/97 AD 09/14/98
          FC EDUC98    97/98 CUR usd AMT       CN 001 XPM a L3/4      ps
    002 PW C390;JLR;v.55(1998)     INV 70730B836 OOOO          MD 08/05/97
          FC EDUC98    97/98 XC 1222 AMT    30.00 usd PT 1 CN 001 PD     30.00
```

FIGURE 6. The Order/Pay/Receipt Record for the Electronic Version of American Imago Is Linked to the Paper Format Subscription Record by Referring to a Combination Order COMB (002). The L4 Field Is Coded for a Web Subscription.

```
LTUL DONE                                              ADF8063
                                    NOTIS ACQUISITIONS         INIC
    UL SERIALS LC a  41002485  ISSN 0065-860X S/STAT c FREQ q S/T p
   American imago. v. 1-  Nov. 1939- -- <Baltimore, Md., etc.> Johns Hopkins
     University Press <etc.>
   PO : 003ADF8063  03/28/1998 ORDUNIT: SA RECUNIT: SA SCOPE: 2
   VENDOR: JOHNSHOP    ACTINT: 2000 POP: x L1: us   L2:
   VA:


   NV:
   NO: COMB (002);OPR for statistics & info only
     SOURCE:                          REF:
     DIV 001 CCN 002 NOTE: ==1922==;UPDATE Action Date occasionally
                                                    MED:    PCS:
   =>002 2T CN |a elec |k Accessible at E-addresses           ITEMS: 0
   001 BE 1997-              E        0.00 EN 00  MD 03/28/98 AD 09/18/03
       FC          00/00 CUR usd AMT  0.00 CN 001 XPM q L3/4        WS
```

Trial Electronic Subscriptions

Not all trial subscriptions are recognized as such at the outset. The web version of *Science* was enthusiastically used and endorsed by science faculty for several months in 1997. Issues of the web version were available four to five weeks before the paper format was mailed. And then, on August 15, 1997, attempts to make electronic contact failed. Faculty were disappointed and library staff had no immediate answer to the problem. Serials Acquisitions staff summoned *Science* on the web and printed the documentation available, 19 pages in all. It explained a complimentary "preview" subscription was available. But the request forms on the web would not accept and utilize the information we offered. No phone number or electronic subscription cost was included in the web documentation. We called the sponsoring body, the American Association for the Advancement of Science. Their publications office explained they did not yet know how they wanted to charge libraries for subscriptions to electronic *Science*. Users were not notified when the trial subscription was about to end. Access was just denied. A summary of all this information was added to the subscription record for the paper format.

After a trial period of free, unrestricted web access the publisher may limit access to only paper format edition subscribers. Access may continue to be free of cost; however, the publisher may assign a user name and password to each electronic subscription. Does the selector or bibliographer want this information added to the cataloging record? Even if a paid subscription is entered the publisher may require submission of a list of user names and e-mail addresses. They often seem to be "build as you go" situations without much, if any, advance notice.

A CD-ROM may appear providing an electronic cumulation for a title purchased in paper format. Sometimes the selector responsible for the title involved will want the CD version cataloged, and sometimes they will not. Each unannounced, unordered, format surprise must be forwarded to the proper selector for a retention decision. If the product is wanted, the cataloging records will be updated and a receiving record for second format will be created.

CONCLUSION

Are the problems associated with establishing standardized workflow for electronic journals new, or did the staff assigned to serials acquisitions when journals in paper format were first invented flounder a bit trying to determine the best way to establish subscriptions? *The New York Magazine; or Literary Repository*, the first illustrated magazine published in New York, commenced publication in January 1790 in New York City. W. L. Andrews described its subscription rules of more than 200 years ago in *The Bookman*, v. 1, May 1895. "The price to subscribers was fixed at eighteen shillings, payable upon the installation plan, five shillings upon the delivery of the first number, five on the delivery of the sixth, and the remaining eight at the expiration of the year. The generous proposition was also made, that if on delivery of the third number the work should not appear to equal the expectation of any subscriber, it would be at his option to discontinue his subscription under forfeit of the five shillings already paid."[5] The article in *The Bookman* does not explain how payment was to be forwarded to the publisher. However, an editorial in the *Independent*, December 1908, 128 years later, titled "How the subscriptions are handled," describes an attempt in that era to arrange a subscription. "A lady wrote to us complaining that she had sent us a dollar for a six months' subscription and had never heard from us. A careful inquiry revealed she had pinned our address on a dollar bill and dropped it in a post box. A search through our files revealed a tag addressed to us with two pin holes through it and postmarked from the source of trouble."[6] Here is proof that complicated subscription arrangements, as well as perplexities in coordinating arrangements with a publisher existed in the past just as they do in the present. Serials acquisitions has handled combination orders for paper format journals, memberships which provide multiple titles, cumulations of varying length, and titles purchased in multiple formats. They have all become part of the normal routine. Acquiring electronic access is a new experience and the workflow is not yet comfortably established, but it will be.

Figures 1 and 2, presented earlier in this article, explain that it does take additional money to acquire access to important information stored electronically. And it is necessary to record the cost and terms of the purchases. How can it be proved that additional staff time is also required? It seems to be a contradiction in concepts. Electronic anything should be faster! Publishers' advertisements and proposals, so many pages in length, arrive every day in the paper format mail. Information is available on the Internet to review. Articles in professional journals suggest strategies and offer educational vision. A crucial part of the electronic access challenge is to be an informed "travel agent." To gather and assess information requires time. Determining suitable workflow and making the best use of system supplied possibilities for record keeping require time for planning and implementation. It is essential to consult with collection management staff, vendors and publishers. Managing change is a component of all these activities. Time is being invested in the attempt to imagine the future and create accurate methods to track the past.

REFERENCES

1. *American Libraries*, 28, no. 4 (1997): [5].
2. Association for Research Libraries. *ARL Statistics, 1995-1996*, Association for Research Libraries, Washington, DC, 1997: 76.
3. Sewell, Robert G. *Results of the final 1996/97 library materials budget survey of the ALCTS/CMDS/Chief Collection Development Officers of Large Research Libraries Discussion Group*: 1997: 2-3.
4. Gates, Bill, "It's a Wired, Wired World," *May Trends*, 23: 1:2.
5. Andrews, W.L. "The first illustrated magazine published in New York," *The Bookman*, 1, no. 4 (1895): 235.
6. Richardson, Gardner, "How the subscriptions are handled," *The Independent*, 65 (Dec. 1908): 1436.

Information Resources Development for Electronic Publications: An Academic Model

Patricia Promis
Atifa Rawan

SUMMARY. The technological changes and automation opportunities by government and private sectors, changing user needs and expectations, and current economic situations have forced academic institutions to reexamine their collection policies and services. In fiscal year 1995/96 one of the Strategic Objectives at the University of Arizona was to develop a library policy for selecting and acquiring electronic products. The purpose of this paper is to provide an overview of how this policy was developed. This study focuses on the methodology used to gather data from library customers, components of the policy, library organization, and the role of selectors. Other issues include trends and initiatives such as duplication, archives, copyright, licensing, and partnerships affecting electronic resources including government publications. *[Article copies available for a fee from The Haworth Document Delivery Service: 1-800-342-9678. E-mail address: getinfo@haworthpressinc.com]*

INTRODUCTION

Electronic resources are bringing new challenges into the library profession. In general, changes experienced in higher education are impacting

---

Patricia Promis, former Acquisitions Librarian, is Associate Librarian with Social Sciences and Fine Arts Humanities Teams (e-mail: ppromis@bird.library.arizona.edu) and Atifa Rawan, former Documents Librarian, is Full Librarian with Social Sciences Team (e-mail: arawan@bird.library.arizona.edu), both at the University of Arizona Library, Tucson, AZ 85720-0055.

[Haworth co-indexing entry note]: "Information Resources Development for Electronic Publications: An Academic Model." Promis, Patricia, and Atifa Rawan. Co-published simultaneously in *The Acquisitions Librarian* (The Haworth Press, Inc.) No. 21, 1999, pp. 51-69; and: *Periodical Acquisitions and the Internet* (ed: Nancy Slight-Gibney) The Haworth Press, Inc., 1999, pp. 51-69. Single or multiple copies of this article are available for a fee from The Haworth Document Delivery Service [1-800-342-9678, 9:00 a.m. - 5:00 p.m. (EST). E-mail address: getinfo@haworthpressinc.com].

© 1999 by The Haworth Press, Inc. All rights reserved.

academic institutions and particularly academic libraries. Libraries are responding by redefining their collection development policies, focusing their attention on users' needs, and facilitating access to information, especially electronic information. In addition to access, libraries are also reexamining other issues such as packaging, storing and archiving resources and coming up with innovative and creative copying strategies. Forces driving these challenges include:

Users' expectations. In general, library users prefer to have remote, free, and speedy access to the most current information. For example, undergraduate students expect to have immediate access to information. They are ready to accept most of their needed sources via electronic means such as Internet and World Wide Web. Faculty and graduate students prefer their libraries to own and to house these resources. They demand specialized collections and assistance from the library. Because of these expectations, academic libraries are reevaluating their services and collection building activities in innovative ways to bring a balance to this area.

Cost. This is a major factor in selection decisions due to continually shrinking budgets. Cost of subscriptions to journals continues to rise as libraries struggle to accommodate their budgets to their users' demands. However, costs of the technologies used in publishing electronic information such as CD-ROMs have become significantly cheaper. As Katherine Martin states, "one CD-ROM can hold 150,000 pages of information or more. The total cost of that CD-ROM might average $2. The cost of equivalent information on paper might be $1,500 or higher."[1]

Government information. In addition to privately published resources, government departments and agencies under pressure from both the executive and legislative branches are converting their publications to electronic format. In the 1990s the United States government agencies produced more documents in electronic format such as CD-ROMs and Internet access. The role of the United States Government Printing Office (GPO) as standard distribution channel is diminishing as more and more agencies publish in digital formats. These trends bring many new challenges to libraries in regard to how the U.S. government information will be available to them in the future. One advantage of government electronic resources is the expeditious dissemination of information. For example, *Consumer Price Index Detailed Report*, *Commerce Business Daily*, the *Federal Register*, and recently proposed and passed laws are available the day they are produced to users all over the world. Thus, library users do not need to wait for documents to be printed, packed, shipped, mailed, received, processed, and finally shelved in their local libraries.

Another issue is the privatization of government information by all levels of governments. Government agencies are invariably looking for ways to cut their publishing costs. In some cases agencies are turning to the private sector to manage their own information. For example, the Securities and Exchange Commission selected the EDGAR system to manage some of its large filings. This cost-cutting results from a moratorium on new government publications in 1981, which placed new requirements to justify continued distribution of existing titles. Many major titles such as *Annual Survey of Child Nutrition* and *Earned Degrees Conferred in the U.S.* were among the casualties of those cost-cutting initiatives.[2] Because of cost-cutting and downsizing efforts, depository libraries are now forced to pay subscription fees to agencies' Internet databases. Agencies such as the National Technical Information Service (NTIS) are selling certain classes of government-funded research material on a cost-recovery basis. Jay Young, Director of Library Programs Service (LPS), Government Printing Office, in his report at the American Library Association Annual Conference in June 1997, also talked about the growing trend of transferring federal government information from the public domain to private ownership. He gave the example of the *Journal of the National Cancer Institute* (NCI), where ownership was transferred from the NCI to Oxford University Press. The Department of Commerce offers a subscription to STAT-USA (the best source of information on business, trade and economics) on the Internet. Depository libraries are allowed to have only one free subscription and are prohibited from sharing the one password.

Technology. Libraries are facing technical compatibility problems with existing hardware/software applications. At the same time, the incompatibility issue creates extra pressure to anticipate future developments. Other concerns include the availability of technical support and maintenance of the products, reliability of telecommunications and servers, the environmental and spatial requirements for equipment and workstations needed, ease of installation of software/hardware, flexibility for other uses/networking, and security from theft and tampering.

Information explosion. There is a growing need to organize and filter electronic information more efficiently and to offer wider access. Libraries are concerned about the quality of information and how to assess the comprehensiveness and scope of the topical and chronological coverage of databases. In addition, accuracy of the data, indexing, ease of use, including products accessed over the Internet, are other matters of concern.

User knowledge. College students and junior faculty are more computer literate today. They are accustomed to more sophisticated electronic software and hardware applications. Thus, their demands for and usage of electronic resources are emerging as a new set of challenges for libraries and librarians.

One way the University of Arizona Library addresses issues such as these is by appointing special project teams. The following study describes steps taken by the University of Arizona Library to develop a policy regarding access and ownership of electronic resources.

THE UNIVERSITY OF ARIZONA LIBRARY MODEL

The University of Arizona is a land-grant research I public institution with an annual budget of $900 million, a student population of 35,000, and 15,000 faculty and staff. Its various programs offer doctoral degrees in 95 fields in the social sciences, sciences, humanities, health sciences, education, business, agriculture, law and fine art disciplines. Particularly strong programs are Astronomy, Optical Sciences, Arid Lands, and Southwest Studies (Borderlands). In addition, the UA is committed to providing strong support for undergraduate curricular activities.

The University of Arizona Library is located in Tucson, 60 miles from the Mexican border with a metropolitan population reaching 800,000. The 1995-96 ARL Index ranks the UA Library in 27th place.

Library Facts[3]

Collections:
Strengths mirror the campus' programmatic emphasis.
Size: 4,001,437 volumes (FY 1996-97)
Current Serials, Including Periodicals Purchased (FY 1996-97): 15,558
Microform Units (FY 1996-97): 4,881,103

Budget (FY 1996/97)	
Total Information Access Budget:	$ 6,161,330
Monographs Expenditures	$ 2,092,546
Serials Expenditures	$ 2,792,367
Other (including Misc.)	$ 1,276,417
Computer files and Search Services are included in the last category ($322,038)	

The University of Arizona Library is a selective depository for federal documents, full depository for European Union documents, and it has a strong collection of UN documents, Arizona state, county and local publications and Southwestern material. For example, Special Collections and the

Southwest Folklore Center house extensive research material on Arizona, the Southwest and the US/Mexico borderlands along with other unique collections such as Morris Udall archival collection. Additionally, the Library has built a World Wide Web site featuring unique visual and archival collections. This site (http://128.196.228.12/libresources/library_www.html) includes highlights from the Center for Creative Photography's collection and a preview of the current exhibitions.

Organizational Structure

The UA Library staff is composed of 296 full time equivalent staff. Of these, 70 are professional staff, 148 support staff and 78 student assistants.[4] In 1993, the library started the process of internal reorganization. The new structure called for a radical shift in focus from a collection-centered library to a customer-centered institution where customers will become self-sufficient in seeking information.

To respond to this new paradigm, a number of teams were established; library activities, functions and services were reorganized and assigned to specific teams. The UA Library currently comprises 11 teams, also referred to as functional teams.[5] Aside from these functional teams, several cross-functional teams were created. The cross-functional teams do not have permanent members. Their members are appointed by the administrative group (Library's Cabinet) or by the individual's hometeam. All teams consist of both professional and classified staff members. All teams report to the Library Cabinet on a regular basis.

Organization for Information Resources Development and Selection

Selection of library materials in all formats, including electronic resources, is the responsibility of selectors. Selectors are librarians belonging to those functional teams that deal directly with the academic programs and teaching faculty (Integrative Services Teams). The body responsible for allocating the Information Access budget and for developing guidelines and policies for these activities in the library is the Information Resources Development and Preservation Council (IRD/P Council). This cross-functional team is also responsible for facilitating the work of selectors through training on issues related to budget management.

In addition to individual teams' ongoing activities, the Library engages in a yearly strategic planning process where projects are identified and prioritized for the coming fiscal year, based on the University's strategic priorities.

Project Development

One of the long-range strategic goals identified by the Library is Access, or more specifically, to improve access to information. To address issues impacting access, each year the Library identifies specific projects. For FY 1995/96 one of the strategic objectives (SOS) was to develop a library policy for selecting and acquiring electronic products.

The University of Arizona Library has a collection of over 8 million items (including microform units) and offers access to more than 1,600 databases plus access to Internet World Wide Web. Through SABIO, the Library's Information System gateway, library customers can access the Internet, World Wide Web sites and databases around the world. The complexity of this area has forced the Library to establish parameters for selecting, acquiring, organizing, and accessing electronic resources.

To accomplish this annual project, four members (including the authors of this article) were appointed from various stakeholder teams in the Library. Members brought a wide spectrum of expertise in the areas of library operations relevant to electronic information technologies and resources, collection development, and acquisitions issues and activities. The team was charged to develop a policy to improve access to electronic resources which would satisfy all reasonable information needs and support collaborative and individual learning and research.

Methodology

1. *Current Situation Analysis.* The first task the team took on was the assessment of the environment. The group used the "situation analysis" method by studying the state, university, library and current trends in academic libraries impacting this issue. The team reviewed existing guidelines for the allocation and management of the information access budget, the current collection development policy, the Strategic Plan Documents for 1996/97, and other relevant documentation from various teams. This included the criteria for purchasing CD-ROMs, criteria for CD-ROM inclusion in the LAN, evaluation of CD-ROMs by subject selectors, the Library's government electronic products, and monographic CD-ROM circulation. In addition, the team closely examined the *Guide to Selecting and Acquiring CD-ROMs, Software and Other Electronic Publications*.[6]
2. *Database Creation.* The team compiled two lists of databases. The first one included government document resources received as depository items. A second list, generated by the Library's Information Access Team (responsible for acquisitions, document delivery and ILL), contained currently owned or newly acquired electronic sources. The latter list was organized by broad subjects such as social sciences, sciences and engineering, fine arts and humanities. The list included general and interdisciplinary sources.
3. *Survey Design and Implementation.* The project team designed a survey to obtain more specific data from selectors. The list created by IAT

needed updating and reevaluation. This survey solicited information on individual databases, current status (received/not received) and location (included current location and preferred location), priority in terms of demand by customers (i.e., 1 = high , 2 = medium, 3 = low), duplication and overlap with currently owned resources, and other pertinent information. The survey was then distributed to all selectors who gathered most accurate and up-to-date data in their respective areas of responsibility. (See Appendix.)
4. *Survey Analysis.* The data from the returned surveys was entered into a relational database. The database allowed the project team to analyze the information in various ways, generating a variety of reports to guide selector's decisions.
5. The next steps for the team were to review the relevant literature and to arrange for visits by vendor's representatives. For example, a visit by the RLG representative was arranged to examine RLG electronic services and resources.
6. *Information Sharing.* The team held two open informational meetings for selectors, to discuss the project team's draft policy. In addition, the draft document was disseminated via electronic mail to all selectors for further input.

Output

The policy was finalized and presented in June 1996 to the entire library staff. As of the new fiscal year (July 1, 1996), the document became the Library's working *Policy for Acquiring and Selecting Electronic Products.*

The policy is divided into five major components. The first section explains basic premises such as current guidelines for budget allocation, issues dealing with remote access and archival copies, and duplication and overlap of resources. The second part establishes the selection criteria and its focus on customer needs, cost considerations, quality of the product, service concerns, and technical concerns. The third section of the policy describes the benefits and limitation of various access options including the World Wide Web, fee-based services, CD-ROM LAN or single machine access, and locally mounted databases. The remaining two sections discuss training, marketing, evaluation and assessment of electronic resources, copyright issues impacting electronic resources, lease and purchase agreement, and licensing. A complete copy of this policy is available online.[7]

Outcome

Full implementation of this policy has been intricate due to several factors. For instance, the policy stresses that the library will fund any information source in only one format. Formats include print, CD-ROM, microform, electronic tape load, gateways, etc. The factors influencing these difficulties are addressed below.

ISSUES

A. Duplication. One of the most difficult tasks is to eliminate or even reduce duplicate copies of the same title in different format. Usually one of the formats in question is digital. What makes this task more difficult is the fact that no two formats contain precisely the same information. The issue of duplicate copies of the same title was addressed when the UA Library went through the major serial subscriptions' cancellation project in FY 1992/93. The accessibility of many resources in electronic format has exacerbated the duplication problem. With full-text services such as *Expanded Academic Index*, the Library is greatly enhancing access to resources to the undergraduate population. However, the institution is paying more than once for the same title, but not always for the same product. Some compromise needs to be achieved between the library and the faculty through extensive negotiation and education processes. A good model is the one followed by Louisiana State University described by Kleiner and Hamaker.[8] At LSU, three projects were aggressively pursued with the goal of containing serials inflation and at the same time expanding the resources available to their community of users.

B. Incompleteness and unreliability of products. According to Carol Tenopir a very limited portion of the scholarly material is available in electronic format. Consequently, libraries are not ready to replace printed journals. What is available varies in quality, accessibility, and price. In addition, an electronic "equivalent" of a print title may be less complete than print, excluding letters-to-editor and other material. Further, Tenopir quotes Ruth Pagell saying "the situation has gotten more complicated because there are so many competing electronic full-text products on so many distribution media. Librarian's role as serials selectors now includes decisions on content, medium, pricing policy, and weighing complex alternatives."[9]

The electronic medium is continuously evolving. New features are constantly developed and implemented through new releases. For example, a common practice among publishers is to offer electronically partial issues of a journal where important pieces are omitted. In these cases, the electronic version is not the same product as the paper counterpart. Commercial publishers are more concerned about offering current information rather than archiving back issues of journals.

The lack of standardized database management software for government information products creates yet another obstacle. The issue of reliability and who generates this electronic information and the dependability of URL addresses are problems which all depository libraries are encountering today.[10]

A related concern is the absence of a reliable mechanism to protect the authenticity of the information. In the electronic environment, products can be easily altered and the authenticity of the version at hand would be difficult to determine. As a result, experimentation and instability are primary characteristics of this medium and libraries need to make timely adjustments to accommodate this situation to serve their customers' needs.

Depository libraries are already facing these dilemmas. Government information in electronic format is not fully reliable and will not completely replace the printed format. For instance, the 1960 Census of Population tapes are now unreadable and libraries depend only on the printed volumes. This forces academic libraries to own or to have access to both formats. Print is still the only reliable long-term storage device and both print and maybe even microfilm will remain readable for many more years. We are not certain if CD-ROMs, floppy disks, and Internet resources produced today will be available to researchers in the future.

C. *Archival issues.* The UA Library policy emphasizes access over ownership. Selectors are encouraged to prefer remote and broader access whenever possible for ease of use and possible cost savings over local maintenance, archiving and storage. For instance, the policy stresses that it is not necessary for the library to own the archival version of the electronic journals. However, ownership can be crucial in certain cases, such as when vendors/publishers do not guarantee the availability of archival copies of those titles considered essential to the research and teaching needs of the university community. Government information available on Internet today is rapidly gone tomorrow. Commercial companies and government agencies have minimal funding for and little interest in long-term maintenance and availability of government research information. Libraries have an important role not only in making current information available but also in preserving information for the future. The National Archives and Records Administration, the agency responsible for preserving the government's permanent records, has been overwhelmed by electronic records because of the amount of information being produced. They do not have the budget or the staffing to keep up with the rapid growth of government's permanent records. Libraries cannot rely on electronic formats alone; they have to select duplicate formats in order to maintain a complete collection of these resources.

One alternative to dealing with archival material has been to create a consortium that shares the high costs of staffing and maintaining the electronic files. An example is the Committee on Institutional Cooperation network (CICNet) project in which a large group of academic libraries are collaborating to archive and to offer access to freely-available electronic journals.

Another example of a consortium effort in academic libraries is *JSTOR* which presents an attractive alternative to archiving electronic journals for a fee.

Another option favored by a large number of libraries is to point to titles which have established a reputation for stability and integrity of their archives on the Internet. The problem with this option is the frequent unavailability (downtime) of the servers offering these archives. Changes of sites' addresses is another common problem encountered with this access option.

Many libraries prefer to archive materials produced locally. The digitized version of local archives is being offered through the Internet. The University of Arizona Library produces archives of the following titles: *Journal of Political Ecology* (University of Arizona, Bureau of Applied Research in Anthropology); *Southwest Institute for Research on Women* (SIROW), via gopher; *Southwest Jewish History* (University of Arizona, Bloom Southwest Jewish Archives).

D. Copyright. This is one of the trickiest issues facing libraries today. An excellent summary of the current state of the copyright and fair use issues is available in the June 97 issue of the *ARL Newsletter*. The entire issue is devoted to this topic with the goal of promoting "the development of consensus within the educational community (defined broadly to include educational authors, rightsholders, and users) around the kind of practices in digital environments that are understood to represent responsible applications of copyright, especially fair use and other educational and library provisions in the law."[11] Library literature carries extensive discussion on this topic with several guides available online.

Many institutions are creating guidelines for fair use and educational copying. To deal with this influx of copyright issues, the University of Arizona Library has created a temporary half-time professional position for the purpose of consulting with faculty regarding curriculum-related copyright issues; educating the library staff as well as the University community on fair use practices in the digital environment; and assisting in shaping University policies relating to scholarly communication, copyright and fair use.

E. Licensing and leasing. A large number of publishers are restricting the use of their products through licensing agreements. These contracts can be extremely elaborate. It is the responsibility of library staff to be cognizant of the limitations imposed by the publisher and to be able to negotiate special clauses more appropriate to their own needs. Before signing any license contract, it is important to be aware of implications such as restrictions on mode of access, conversion of data, restrictions on type of users allowed, limited capabilities for downloading and transferring information.

Numerous articles discussing these issues are available in the professional literature. Helpful assistance for librarians dealing with license agreements can be found online through Liblicense.[12] Another rich online source is

Licensing Electronic Information. This web site is maintained by the Association of Research Libraries.[13]

TRENDS AND NEW INITIATIVES

Organizational Changes

The current literature offers several accounts in which libraries present their organizational models. Some libraries are integrating their format-oriented units such as media, maps, and documents into one centralized area of service.

Other libraries are now distributing work activities based on holistic approaches. In the collection development arena, a standard arrangement in academic libraries is a separate unit, committee or department whose members are bibliographers. These collection development groups are making all collection-related decisions, not always with input from selectors. The current trend is to involve the individuals (selectors, subject specialists) who perform selection in the decision-making process. This is the model the University of Arizona Library is implementing. Kleiner and Hamaker also mention the need to involve selectors at LSU in collection development efforts.[14]

Samuel Demas describes an interesting organizational model developed at Cornell University's Mann Library that allows for the integration of systematic selection of electronic publications into their collection development program. In implementing this new model they have introduced the concepts of information genres, genre specialist, and tiers of access.[15]

Initiatives Related to Government Information

1. Depository libraries are allocating additional resources in the digital environment. In addition to terminals and access to Internet, libraries are downloading very large files on faster and more reliable software/hardware applications. Some agency publications also require the purchase of costly commercial software such as Geographic Information System (GIS). And some electronic government documents cannot be reproduced without fast printing capabilities.

2. Libraries are integrating their government documents services and activities. They are no longer able to maintain a separate unit and be self-sufficient with their computer hardware and software equipment and staffing.

3. Depository libraries are reexamining their item selection policies and depository status. It is expensive to be a regional or a large selective deposito-

ry. Sandy Housley conducted an informal survey of depository libraries via an electronic distribution listserv (GOVDOC-L) in December of 1996. She received 15 responses (11 academic, 3 public, and one state library). Based on her sample survey it was interesting to know that the average cost of a depository title is $11.

4. Government Partnerships. Government agencies are attempting to provide free access to their electronic resources. Examples of such efforts include:

A report produced by GPO staff in June 15, 1997, estimates that more than 50% of all tangible government information products are not available to depository libraries. The majority of these (55,000) reports are scientific and technical documents. If that many sci-tech documents were in paper format, GPO and libraries could not handle them. Through partnership initiatives it is possible to disseminate this large body of information in the Federal Depository Library Program for the first time. For example, NTIS is working with UC-Davis on a "pre-pilot" project to enable depositories to have access to NTIS electronic image files free of charge.[16]

Another initiative is the interagency agreement between GPO and National Commission on Libraries and Information Science (NCLIS) to establish and to conduct an assessment of standards for creation, dissemination, and permanent accessibility of electronic government information products. The project is not ready for GPO to pilot yet. However, an agreement in principle has been made between ERIC, OCLC, and GPO, under which OCLC will maintain and make available to depositories the public domain ERIC reports.

Members of the library community and GPO have partnered on a legislative initiative to change the existing laws relating to federal information in electronic form. In 1997, the American Library Association organized an inter-association working group and drafted a legislative proposal to amend the Depository Library Act (44 USC 19). The proposal was delivered to Congress in early June and included a draft bill entitled *Federal Information Access Act of 1997*. This draft proposes a comprehensive rewrite of chapter 19, which deals with the federal information access program in the electronic age.[17]

Other efforts are being undertaken by the Department of Education (ERIC) and the National Library of Medicine (NLM). NLM is providing depository libraries with free access to its database, Internet Grateful Med (IGM), which allows access to its popular database MEDLINE. ERIC is building an electronic system which makes it possible to have access to its bibliographic file.

In addition to the efforts undertaken by government agencies, private and commercial publishers are also partnering with libraries. According to Kit Kennedy, "resource sharing is the patriarch of partnership."[18] Libraries have always been involved in collaborative endeavors but now they are exploring more creative and cost-effective methods to deal with the electronic environment.

Libraries are developing partnership projects among them. For example, the University of Arizona Library is developing consortia efforts with various partners, depending on the product. One consortium includes Arizona academic libraries. Another effort is between the University of Arizona Library, a public library and a community college library for a combined subscription to *Encyclopedia Britannica Online*.

CONCLUSION

The electronic environment is forcing librarians to work more collaboratively and to consult with other specialists throughout the decision-making process. Libraries are now forced to keep up with the hardware and software required to access materials. In doing so, libraries are producing new sets of documents and policies to guide their decisions.

Along with policies, libraries are also looking into other creative ways to continue their high level of service to their users. Costs of electronic products are prohibitive, and therefore, partnerships offer an alternative for providing access to information.

All these efforts along with budgetary constraints are moving the libraries and the profession in new directions. Libraries cannot afford to continue to have highly specialized librarians. Instead, librarians are expected to know about new and existing technology, services, collections, resource sharing, teaching methodologies, and vendor relationships in order to satisfy the demands and needs of their customers.

Laverna Saunders in her chapter "The Evolving Virtual Library: An Overview"[19] identifies eight trends in libraries in the 1990s: More and more libraries offering their catalogs online; the digital library offering full-text electronic resources; libraries offering gateway systems where the online catalog is just one of the options; the dramatic move towards electronic journals and the increase in electronic publishing activities; the heavy use of document delivery services as a way to expand "collections"; the integration of resources available on Internet to the "collection"; multimedia integration; and end-user empowerment. She concludes by saying that "the benefit of the virtual library is increase in access, not reduced costs."[20]

Michael Gorman in his article titled "Ownership and Access: A New Idea of 'Collection' " discusses four main components for a modern library collection. According to him, these components are "tangible objects" and "intangible electronic documents." "Tangible objects" are owned and available in-house, where the "intangible electronic documents" could be available via interlibrary loan and other resource-sharing methods electronically for a fee or without a fee. He then challenges libraries by asking "Are we up to the challenge of extending that bibliographic control and preservation to electronic documents?" He further adds it is possible "if libraries have the necessary determination, organization and confidence."[21] In a separate work, Gorman and Crawford discuss the importance of adopting and maintaining the balance between collection and access. According to them, the future means both print and electronic communication; linear text and hypertext; mediation by librarians and direct access; collections and access and a library that is both edifice and interface. [22]

REFERENCES

1. Katherine Martin, "Understanding the Forces For and Against Electronic Information Publishing: It's Six of One, Half-dozen of the Other." *CD-ROM Professional* 7, no. 4 (July/August 1994): 129.

2. Katherine F. Mawdsley (1997, July 30) "Access to Government Information in Electronic Format: The Librarian's Perspective" [online]. Available www://http://www.cpsr.org/dox/conferences/cfp91/mawdsley.html.

3. University of Arizona (1997, August 12) "The Statistical Yellow Pages," in *General Information About the Library* [online]. Available www://http://dizzy.library.arizona.edu/y-pages/welcome.html.

4. Ibid.

5. For a more detailed description of individual teams, see Appendix: University of Arizona Library Organization in: Patricia Promis, "Developing a Databased Budget Allocation Strategy: The University of Arizona Library Experience." *Collection Building* 15, no. 3 (1996): 9.

6. Stephen Bosch, Patricia Promis and Chris Sugnet, *Guide to Selecting and Acquiring CD-ROMs, Software, and Other Electronic Publications* (Chicago: American Library Association, 1994).

7. The University of Arizona Library (1997, August 29) "The University of Arizona Library Policy for Selecting and Acquiring Electronic Products," in Sabio [online]. Available www://http://dizzy.library.arizona.edu/library/teams/iat/elecpub.htm.

8. Jane P. Kleiner and Charles Hamaker, "Libraries 2000: Transforming Libraries Using Document Delivery, Needs Assessment, and Networked Resources." *College & Research Libraries* 58, no. 4 (July 1997): 355-374.

9. Carol Tenopir, "The Complexities of Electronic Journals." *Library Journal* 122, no. 2 (February 1997): 37.

10. Judy Andrews (1997, July 30) "Government Information in an Electronic Age" [online]. Available www://http://www.ala.org/acrl/paparhtm/a08.html.

11. "Copyright and Fair Use in Digital Environments: Challenges for the Educational Community." *ARL: A Bimonthly Newsletter of Research Library Users and Actions. Special Issue* 192 (June 1997): 1.

12. Yale University Library (1997, August 11) "Liblicense: Licensing Digital Information. A Resource for Librarians," in *Liblicense: Licensing Digital Information* [online]. Available: http://www.library.yale.edu/~llicense/index.shtml.

13. Patricia Brennan, Karen Hersey and Georgia Harper (1997, August 11) "Strategic and Practical Considerations for Signing Electronic Information Delivery Agreements," in *Licensing Electronic Resources* [online]. Available www://http://arl.cni.org/scomm/licensing/licbooklet.html.

14. Kleiner and Hamaker, *Libraries 2000*.

15. Samuel Demas, "Collection Development for the Electronic Library: A Conceptual and Organizational Model." *Library Hi Tech* 12, no. 3 (1994): 71-80.

16. United States Government Printing Office, "Fugitive Documents: Scope and Solutions." *Administrative Notes* (June 15, 1997).

17. American Library Association (1997, June 30) "Issue Brief" [online]. Available www://http://www.ala.org/washoff/fdlp.html.

18. Kit Kennedy, "Emerging Patterns of Partnership in Collection Development: A Subscription Vendor's Perspective." *Journal of Library Administration* 24, no. 1/2 (1997): 104.

19. Laverna Saunders, "The Evolving Virtual Library: An Overview," in *The Evolving Virtual Library: Information in Electronic Format: The Librarian's Visions and Case Studies* (Medford, NJ: Information Today, Inc., 1996): 1-16.

20. Ibid. p. 9.

21. Michael Gorman, "Ownership and Access: A New Idea of 'Collection'." *College & Research Libraries News* 58, no. 7 (1997): 498-499.

22. Walt Crawford and Michael Gorman, *Future Libraries: Dreams, Madness and Reality* (Chicago: American Library Association, 1995).

BIBLIOGRAPHY

Brichford, Maynard and William Maher. "Archival Issues in Network Electronic Publications." *Library Trends* 43 (Spring 1995): 701-712.

Cochenour, Donnice. "CICNet's Electronic Journal Collection." *Serials Review* 22 (Spring 1996): 63-69.

Cochenour, Donnice. "Relying on the Kindness of Strangers: Archiving Electronic Journals on Gopher." *Serials Review* 21, no. 1 (1995): 67-77.

"Copyright and Fair Use in Digital Environments: Challenges for the Educational Community." *ARL: A Bimonthly Newsletter of Research Library Issues and Actions* 192, Special Copyright Issue (June 1997): 1-16.

Cornwell, Gary et al., "Problems and Issues Affecting the U.S. Depository Library Program and the GPO: The Librarians' Manifesto." *Government Publications Review* 20 (1993): 121-140.

Crawford, Walt and Michael Gorman. *Future Libraries: Dreams, Madness, and Reality*. Chicago: American Library Association, 1995.

Davis, Tricia L. "License Agreements in Lieu of Copyright: Are We Signing Away Our Rights?" *Library Acquisitions: Practice & Theory* 21, no. 1 (1997): 19-27.

DeGennaro, Richard. "JSTOR: The Vanguard of the Retrospective Digital Library." *Library Issues: Briefings for Faculty and Administrators* 17, no. 4 (March 1997).

Demas, Samuel. "Collection Development for the Electronic Library: A Conceptual and Organizational Model." *Library Hi Tech* 12, no. 3 (1994): 71-80.

Demas, Samuel, Peter McDonald and Gregory Lawrence. "The Internet and Collection Development: Mainstreaming Selection of Internet Resources." *LRTS* 39, no. 3 (1995): 275-290.

Dickinson, Dennis. "Copyright Dilemma: The Need for Local Policy." *Library Issues: Briefings for Faculty and Administrators* 16, no. 4 (March 1996): 1-2.

Electronic Journals in ARL Libraries: Issues and Trends. Compiled by Elizabeth Parang and Laverna Saunders. Washington, DC: Association of Research Libraries, 1994.

Electronic Journals in ARL Libraries: Policies and Procedures. Compiled by Elizabeth Parang and Laverna Saunders. Washington, DC: Association of Research Libraries, 1994.

Fales, Susan L., ed. *Guide for Training Collection Development Librarians.* Chicago: American Library Association, 1996.

Ferguson, Anthony W. "Interesting Problems Encountered On My Way to Writing an Electronic Information Collection Development Statement." *Against the Grain* 7, no. 2 (April 1995): 16-19.

Gorman, Michael. "Ownership *and* Access: A New Idea of 'Collection'." *College & Research Library News* 58, no. 7 (July/August 1997): 498-499.

Harter, Stephen P. "Accessing Electronic Journals and Other E-publications: An Empirical Study." *College and Research Libraries* 57, no. 5 (September 1996): 440-456.

Jacob, Herbert. "The Future is Electronic." *Social Science Quarterly* 77, no. 1 (March 1996): 204-209.

Kennedy, Kit. "Emerging Patterns of Partnership in Collection Development: A Subscription Vendor's Perspective." *Journal of Library Administration* 24, nos. 1-2 (1997): 103-111.

Kleiner, Jane P. "Libraries 2000: Transforming Libraries Using Document Delivery, Needs Assessment, and Networked Resources." *College and Research Libraries* 58, no. 4 (July 1997): 355-374.

Lenzini, Rebecca T. "New Partners for Collection Development." *Journal of Library Administration* 24, nos. 1-2 (1997): 113-123.

Martin, Katherine. "Understanding the Forces for and Against Electronic Information Publishing: It's Six of One, Half-dozen of the Other." *CD-Rom Professional* 7, no. 4 (July-August 1994): 129-134.

Massant, Eric J. "The Roles of Libraries and the Private Sector: Policy Principles for Assuring Public Access to U.S. Federal Government Information: A Viewpoint." *Journal of Government Information* 22, no. 5 (1994): 383-390.

Metz, Paul. "Serials Pricing and the Role of the Electronic Journal." *College and Research Libraries* 52, no. 4 (July 1991): 315-327.

Miller, Rachel. "Emerging Patterns of Collection Development in an Expanding Resource Sharing, Electronic Information, and Network Environment: Report of a Conference." *Library Acquisitions: Practice & Theory* 21, no. 2 (1997): 211-219.

Miller, William. "Government Documents and Libraries: The Impact of the Digital Revolution." *Library Issues* 17, no. 4 (March 1997): 1-3.

Report of the Task Force on Archiving Digital Information: Preserving Digital Information. May 1, 1996. John Garret and Donald Waters, co-chairs.

Saunders, Laverna M., ed. *The Evolving Virtual Library: Visions and Case Studies.* Medford, NJ: Information Today, Inc., 1996.
Strategic Long Range Planning Team Current Situation Analysis Subteam. *The University of Arizona Libraries: Current Situation Analysis for 1996/97.* University of Arizona, October-November 1995.
Tenopir, Carol. "The Complexities of Electronic Journals." *Library Journal* 122, no. 2 (February 1997): 37-39.

INTERNET RESOURCES

- ARL. Preserving Digital Information at <http://www.rlg.org/ArchTF/tfadi.index.htm#contents>
- ARL. Licensing Electronic Resources at <http://arl.cni.org/scomm/licensing/licbooklet.html>
- The Copyright Website at <http://www.benedict.com/home.htm>
- Guidelines for Appropriate Use of MIT's Campus Wide Information Systems at <http://web.mit.edu/cwis/www/faq/guidelines.html>
- SUL: Copyright and Fair Use at <http://fairuse.stanford.edu/>
- National Humanities Alliance. Basic Principles for Managing Intellectual Property in the Digital Environment at <http://www-ninch.cni.org/ISSUES/COPYRIHT/PRINCIPLES/NHA_Complete.html>
- Principles for Licensing Electronic Resources at <http://arl.cni.org/scomm/licensing/principles.html>
- Strategic and Practical Considerations for Signing Electronic Information Delivery Agreements at <http://arl.cni.org/scomm/licensing/licbooklet.html>
- University of California Library. Principles for Acquiring and Licensing Information in Digital Format at <http://sunsite.berkeley.edu/Info/principles.html>
- The UT System Crash Course in Copyright at <http://www.utsystem.edu/OGC/IntellectualProperty/cprtindx.htm>
- Yale University Library. Liblicense: Licensing Digital Information at <http://www.library.yale.edu/~llicense/index.shtml>

APPENDIX

Electronic Product Survey for Selectors

The Strategic Objectives 2 project teams for Resources and for Tools need information from selectors to inform our Current Situation Analysis (CSA). The information you provide will help us in our objectives to reduce duplication and provide hardware and software framework to serve us now and in the future. Please take the time to review and annotate the accompanying lists and return by November 17 to our contact person(s).

1. Databases: Attached you will find 2 lists of electronic products we have identified as being either owned or ordered by the Library. Please identify those titles that you consider to be primarily from your assigned subject areas. Indicate these on the Survey Answer Form under column 1 by section and item number (e.g., Fine Arts/Humanities, #3), not by writing out the titles elsewhere.
2. Priority: Within the titles in your subject area(s) that you have already listed, please indicate a priority (#1 being highest priority) for customer availability in column 6 on the answer sheet.
3. Duplication: In column 3 note any duplication of the *exact title* in other formats. Please indicate differences between formats in regard to coverage, etc.
   Please indicate if the title is available in another format, please list title(s) and format(s) on the answer sheet. Formats might include: Internet, FirstSearch, Dialog, paper, microform, dial-up via modem, Sabio, CD-ROM LAN, CD-ROM single use station, QuickSearch, other.
4. Content/Overlap: Please note databases that we presently own or have ordered that OVERLAP significantly in subject coverage. Also note any overlap with paper, electronic information on the Internet, etc., that you are aware of.
5. Location: Do you have a specific means-of-access or location in mind (according to the criteria for CD-ROM inclusion on the LAN-attached)?
   Please identify the best possible access mode for each of the titles in your area:

Short term circulation	LAN
Long term circulation	Dial-up via modem
Sabio	Internet (with password)
Single-use station	

6. Information: In column 2, please provide us with any information you may have (e.g., subscription, number of discs, frequency, etc.) on these titles. If you have additional information (publishers flyers, e-mail printouts, etc.) either attach copies to the form or indicate that you have additional information in column 2 and we will contact you for it.

Electronic Product Survey Answer Sheet

Name: Team:

1. Databases	2. Priority			3. Duplication	4. Overlap	5. Location	6. Information
	1	2	3				

Government Serials on the Internet: Challenges and Opportunities

Ted D. Smith

SUMMARY. This article reviews the rapid transition of government serials toward online access and surveys current problems this evolution is causing for libraries trying to provide access to the data. Government serials have a number of characteristics that have made them a thorny problem for libraries, and in some ways online access may be worsening the situation. Both libraries and library users face some significant challenges and increased costs associated with government serials in the electronic environment. Yet, there is hope that the continual evolution toward online access will at long last provide more complete access to these traditionally under-utilized resources. *[Article copies available for a fee from The Haworth Document Delivery Service: 1-800-342-9678. E-mail address: getinfo@haworthpressinc.com]*

INTRODUCTION

The remarkable rise of the Internet as an information dissemination tool over the past several years has greatly affected society in many ways. This information revolution has had a profound impact on many professions, perhaps none more so than the field of librarianship. The development of computer-based online systems has been both a boon and a bane to those of us whose work involves helping others locate needed information, as it provides both a heightened degree of access and unparalleled challenges in

---

Ted D. Smith is Documents Reference Librarian, University of Oregon Library, Eugene, OR 97403-1299.

[Haworth co-indexing entry note]: "Government Serials on the Internet: Challenges and Opportunities." Smith, Ted D. Co-published simultaneously in *The Acquisitions Librarian* (The Haworth Press, Inc.) No. 21, 1999, pp. 71-81; and: *Periodical Acquisitions and the Internet* (ed: Nancy Slight-Gibney) The Haworth Press, Inc., 1999, pp. 71-81. Single or multiple copies of this article are available for a fee from The Haworth Document Delivery Service [1-800-342-9678, 9:00 a.m. - 5:00 p.m. (EST). E-mail address: getinfo@haworthpressinc.com].

managing the flood of information. While all aspects of information access have undergone profound changes as a result, perhaps none has evolved quite so rapidly as has the publication of government serials. A challenge to libraries in the most quiescent of times, government serials have lately become even more problematic due to the current brisk pace of technological change.

Government serials have a number of characteristics that have always made them difficult to bring under bibliographic control. To begin with, their publication is a by-product of the governing and policy-making process, not an end in itself as with most commercially produced publications. This causes them to have less consistent patterns of publication and makes them more prone to variations in titles, numbering and frequency than commercial titles. Lacking the vendor-customer relationship that exists between a commercial publisher and its subscribers, the authoring agency of a government periodical may feel less of an obligation to adhere to strict schedules of publication and distribution. Many libraries obtain government serials by virtue of participation in various depository arrangements, so even the method of acquisition often differs from that used for other types of periodicals. This creates added difficulties in locating and claiming missing issues. The fact that the distributing agency is not the agency that actually publishes the serial means that it is frequently necessary to have special procedures in place to claim copies from either the depository agency or the publishing agency, depending on the particular circumstance.[1]

Even before the advent of online networks, the distribution of government serials had undergone a series of difficult transitions. Beginning in the 1970s, the United States Government Printing Office (G.P.O.) embarked on a program of converting many publications to microfiche format for distribution to depository libraries. This format change necessitated additional cataloging by libraries seeking to adhere to the standard of creating separate catalog records for different formats. Unfortunately, the problem often was not limited to a one-time change. Despite a stated policy that a decision to distribute a serial in microfiche will apply to all future issues,[2] in practice the distribution of government serials has sometimes varied between print and microfiche from one issue to another. Furthermore, it is not uncommon for claimed copies of missing issues to be received in a different format than the regular distribution. This is particularly true in cases in which it is necessary to claim the missing issue from the publishing agency rather than the G.P.O.

During the 1980s a significant number of United States government serials were discontinued as a result of budget cutting measures.[3] As governments at all levels have had to deal with increasing fiscal constraints over the past two decades, many serial titles have undergone downsizing, merging with other titles and cessation of publication.

As the widespread availability of personal computer technology worked its changes on society in the 1980s and 1990s, the same need for cost-cutting efficiencies that drove the earlier transitions caused government publishers to be among the first to adopt new electronic methods of distribution. As early as 1984, the Congressional committee responsible for oversight of the Federal Depository Library Program began to identify government publications that would be appropriate for electronic distribution to depository libraries, many of which were serials.[4] Government serials have proven to be particularly amenable to online distribution. Many are statistical in nature, so that online systems provide users with access to the data in a desirable format that readily allows for user manipulation or analysis. Online publications can be provided in a form that can easily be loaded into spreadsheet programs or other applications software. Other titles, such as the *Congressional Record*, are voluminous records of agency activities that are expensive to publish and distribute in physical formats and for which the full-text searching facilitated by online access is highly desirable. Perhaps the most important incentive of all for rapid implementation of online access (at least insofar as the U.S. federal government is concerned) has been legislative mandate.[5] As Congress has grappled with soaring budget deficits over the past two decades, all discretionary spending, including agency publishing programs and the Government Printing Office's operations, has come under intense scrutiny as a target for potential cost savings. The agencies responsible for the distribution of government information have responded with extensive planning for ways to implement electronic access to information previously published in paper. A major example of such a planning effort is the U.S. Government Printing Office's *Study to Identify Measures Necessary for a Successful Transition to a More Electronic Federal Depository Library Program*.[6]

While the U.S. federal government has been the leader in the transformation to electronic formats, other governments have proceeded with transition programs of their own. The government of Canada has implemented an "Electronic Publications Pilot" (EPP) in which participating libraries have access to selected Statistics Canada and parliamentary publication via the Internet rather than in physical formats. The purpose of this project is to assess the impact on libraries of replacing print publications with electronic equivalents. While, as of this writing, there has been no announcement of the results of the pilot project, clearly the Government of Canada intends to include some increased reliance on the Internet in its mix of information dissemination strategies. Below the national level, state and provincial governments throughout North America now provide access to legislative bills and other official documents via the World Wide Web. The European Union provides access to a number of official publications via Internet-accessible databases, and national level governments throughout the world have established WWW sites to provide access to some of their official publications. In addition to these broad government programs, many individual government agencies have established Internet sites which users from throughout the world can use to access the agencies' official publications.

THE GOVERNMENT PUBLISHER'S PERSPECTIVE

From the point of view of the government publisher, the decision to disseminate information online rather than in a physical format involves an evaluation of the suitability of a given technology to a particular information dissemination problem. In making this choice, the publishing agency ideally will consider several factors, such as the organization's objectives, end-user needs and the characteristics of the service to be provided.[7] At times, however, the issue of cost-effectiveness may become the prime concern that overrides all others. In such cases there is a serious danger that the conversion to Internet access will actually result in decreased access and greater difficulty for libraries. Even if organizational objectives, user needs and service characteristics *are* given serious consideration, the focus is likely to be on the perceived needs of the agency's own clientele, be they government employees or specific groups of citizens. The potential impact on libraries is likely to receive little (if any) consideration.

Even when there are legitimate benefits to be realized from the conversion to online access, much of the cost savings realized by the publishing agency is actually passed on to the end-user or the servicing library. For example, it is certainly true that it costs Statistics Canada less to publish a title such as *Education in Canada* on the Internet rather than printing and distributing paper copies of the publication. However, a library wishing to provide access to the Internet document incurs costs over and above what it would to provide access to the paper copy. A paper copy requires the library to spend money for the staff time to order, process, catalog and maintain the collection, all of which are already built in to the library's operating budget. If the library is not a depository, there may also be a cost incurred in purchasing a subscription to the government serial. To provide access to Internet based materials, libraries must still devote staff resources to identify, catalog and help users locate the online materials. In addition, they must provide the telecommunications link to the Internet and up-to-date computer equipment to access, view and (perhaps) print the publication. What is more, it is highly unlikely (given the current state of video display technology) that viewing a lengthy document on a computer terminal will be acceptable to most users as the only mode of access. Printing of at least some parts of the document is likely to be necessary, either at the user's expense or the library's.

Once an agency has chosen the Internet as the desired method of distribution for a given publication, there is still the matter of choosing the most suitable data format in which to provide the data. The choice the agency makes in this matter can also have serious repercussions, both for the short-term usability of the data and for its long-term viability as a store of archival information. Data may be formatted in a number of ways: in Hypertext Markup Language (HTML), in plain text (ASCII), in comma-delimited or tab-delimited text (to allow for easy loading into spreadsheet or database applications), or in any of a number of proprietary formats (e.g., Adobe's *portable document format*, Lotus spreadsheet format or dBase format). The suitability of a particular format for a given document will depend upon the characteristics of the situation, involving much the same considerations as the initial decision between print and online distribution. If an unsuitable format is chosen it may either make it more difficult for the user to utilize the information or create problems later if the format becomes obsolete.

A TAXONOMY OF FORMAT CONVERSIONS

It is worth noting that the conversion of a serial title to electronic format may take any of a number of different forms. The change may be either part of a large planned conversion (as with *GPO Access* or Canada's EPP), or may be based on an individual decision by a publishing agency. The conversion to electronic format may mean a conversion to a physical computer-readable format such as CD-ROM, or it may mean a switch to online (Internet) access. Conversion to CD-ROM means that it is still necessary to maintain a physical distribution system, while Internet access changes even the mode of transmission. What is more, there are a variety of possible permutations as to the characteristics of the transition:

- A straightforward switch from one format to another: paper publication ceases but the serial continues with the same title and information content in the new, electronic format.
- Publication in both electronic and print formats simultaneously for an indefinite period of time.
- Publication in both electronic and print formats simultaneously for a short transition period, followed by discontinuation of the non-electronic format.
- The data previously published in a given serial made available in electronic form as part of a more comprehensive database or collection, with the previously published government serial no longer being published in any form.
- The data previously published in a given serial becomes part of a more comprehensive database or collection, but the serial continues to be published separately in physical format.

- The government serial converts to electronic format, but is still published in physical format in a reduced or scaled-down version.
- The government serial continues in physical format, but in a greatly reduced or scaled-down version; additional data previously included in the print publication is now available as part of some online database or collection.

ISSUES FOR LIBRARIES

As can be seen from the enumeration of possible variations, libraries seeking to continue to provide access to the information content of government serials face a number of daunting challenges. In some cases the agency may decide to convert the publication to electronic access on the basis of cost savings alone, without regard to whether or not the new format is suitable for the material being converted. In other cases electronic access may provide real benefits to the user, but even in this happy circumstance libraries must still be prepared to deal with a number of difficult issues. Libraries must provide tools and reference assistance for users seeking to locate the data. They also face the challenge of providing continuity between the older material (most often *not* converted to electronic format) and the new computer-based data. These issues bear closer examination, for how libraries resolve them will do much to shape the way in which they will carry out their function in the near future.

The first set of issues falls under the heading of *collection development*. That is, they relate to the question of how the library identifies and "collects" those items that are most appropriate for its users' needs. Presumably, if the library has been receiving the government serial in paper it is a title deemed appropriate for the particular collection. However, such a decision reached in regard to a paper publication may not necessarily hold true for the new electronic version. As can be seen from the taxonomy of format conversions, the content and characteristics of the online version of a given publication might differ substantially from the print version in a number of ways. Take, for example, the case of a publication that has ceased in paper with the previous contents now being provided as part of a large database or collection of information. Such a situation currently exists for the U.S. Department of Commerce's *Overseas Business Reports*, among other publications. Comprehensive research libraries will likely want to retain access to the larger database, and, so long as access is free or provided at very low cost, so will most others. When the agency provides access to the online database on a fee-only basis, a smaller library must consider the cost of providing access to a database that may contain much material that is beyond the scope of its collection.

Another variation is the situation in which the publication is now provided in multiple formats. A current example (again from the U.S. Department of Commerce), is the *Survey of Current Business*, a standard source of information on the U.S. economy in many libraries. It is still being published in paper, but is now also available through the Department of Commerce's *Stat-USA* online service and in annual cumulation as a CD-ROM. Libraries participating in the U.S. Federal Depository Library Program now have access to all three by virtue of their depository status. However, if future policy changes provide for depository access to be in one format only, each depository library will be forced to choose which format is most suitable for its needs. The many non-depository libraries that subscribe to the serial already face these decisions for this important title. There are a number of factors to be considered. Which format best meets the needs of the library's clientele? Is it worth the additional cost to obtain the data in more than one format? Given that online access to the publication is through a more comprehensive set of databases (*Stat-USA*), how do we compare the value of the online product with the value of the more focused print product? What are the prospects for continuation of the print product, and for how long? These can be difficult questions to answer, and as we have seen, libraries may confront these issues and similar issues in a variety of different situations with regard to a publication's conversion.

In view of the complexities, it is important that libraries approach the collection development issues on the basis of established principles rather than trying to deal with each situation *ad hoc*. In this regard, libraries that have a strong collection development policy that has been updated to address issues relating to electronic formats will be in a better position to deal with the complexities than similar institutions lacking such a policy. In evaluating the information content of electronic resources, libraries should consider the same properties and characteristics as for traditional print resources. The primary properties to be addressed will still be the *relevance* of the information for library users, the *quality* of the information provided, and the *timeliness* of the information.[8] The electronic format introduces complexities, however, in that a number of technology-related factors must be taken into account. Issues such as hardware requirements, format of the data, functionality of the software interface, the availability of archival material and mode of access[9] will affect how (indeed whether) the library can provide access to the data.

Perhaps the most vexing collection development issue of all is the essential question of what constitutes the library collection in a distributed information environment. Is it necessary to add a record for an online resource to the library's catalog in order for it to be part of the collection? Does the inclusion of a hyperlink in a web page maintained by the library constitute adding the item to the collection? If so, should the inclusion of such hyperlinks be subjected to the same criteria as adding other materials to the collection?

Some problems in the acquisition of electronic serials are unique to depository libraries. One long-standing issue with depository programs is the number of "fugitive" publications that exist. These are official publications that should be included in the depository distribution system but are (for whatever reason) not captured by the depository agency for distribution. Depository libraries have developed various techniques for handling these items over the years, such as subscribing to commercial services that capture such fugitive publications,[10] contacting agencies directly to get on mailing lists or obtain gift subscriptions and paying for subscriptions. Online access can in some situations make this task easier. Marginal or little-used publications may be accessed on an "as needed" basis rather than acquiring each issue "just-in-case," and publications on the Internet are likely to be easier to locate than are those published in print but not in the library's collection. However, complications can arise. If a publication that formerly came as a print depository item stops coming, some work may be necessary to identify the reason for the cessation. It is possible that the serial has ceased publication, or perhaps it has been converted to online access. If it is online, it might be that the print version is no longer being produced at all, or perhaps it is still possible to obtain a print copy but the depository system is relying on the electronic version for its distribution. As is often the case with online government serials, it is necessary for the library to consider many possibilities in determining what the situation is with a given title and what course of action is needed to maintain the library's collection.

Once the collection development issues have been addressed, a range of *management* issues comes into focus. The need for equipment to provide access is an increasingly large consideration in library budgeting. The U.S. Superintendent of Documents has for many years provided recommended specifications for public access workstations in depository libraries.[11] These guidelines are upgraded on a regular basis to reflect the advance of technology and the increasing need for computing power to access the growing array of electronic information products produced by the government. The need to purchase and maintain state-of-the-art computer hardware puts a severe strain on already stretched library budgets.

Going hand-in-hand with increasing equipment needs is the need for greater and greater levels of technological expertise among librarians and other library staff. Government documents librarians have always needed a specialized expertise in government structure and policy-making procedure. Now they are often called upon to have expert skills in searching online databases, installing search software, creating HTML documents and understanding computer hardware and operating systems as well. It thus becomes increasingly difficult to maintain the skills needed to effectively connect users to the government data they need. Libraries must be prepared to offer service to patrons with a wide variety of skill levels when it comes to computer technology. Sometimes users know their subject but don't understand how to use the technology. Sometimes they are quite savvy about using computers and the Internet, but don't know enough about government to know what they should be looking for. And sometimes they know quite a bit about both policy making processes and the technology, but just cannot quite put their virtual finger on the exact information needed. In each instance, the help of an information professional is the essential ingredient needed to connect citizen to government.

A third major category of issues is that of *access*, especially issues specifically relating to the library catalog. The library must determine the best method for informing users of the existence and availability of an online publication. Is it necessary to add a record for an online resource to the library's catalog? If the decision is "yes," then a myriad of other questions must be addressed. How best to inform users who locate the record for a serial title held in paper that newer editions may be available online (either in addition to or in place of paper copies)? Is it desirable (or even possible) to check-in new editions when they are posted to the Web? One way to handle serials that are available as part of a larger database would be to provide analytic records for individual data series or significant subsets of the database. Another approach might be to develop finding guides posted as Web pages to assist users in locating specific kinds of information. Sometimes decisions will be dictated by the current status of the library's OPAC, i.e., the existence of a Web interface (Webpac) and the capability of a given system for handling hyperlinks and other data specific to electronic resources. While bibliographic standards such as AACR2 and MARC continue to play an important role in the viability of the library catalog and should be respected, providing access to electronic resources may call for some flexibility in our approach. For example, the principle of using distinct bibliographic records for different formats may actually become a barrier to access in an environment in which the format of government serials may differ from one issue to the next. It might also be useful to make more extensive use of notes in bibliographic records to provide users with specific access information concerning online serials, perhaps pointing to guides maintained on the Web that provide more information about the content of large databases.

An alternative to cataloging each title is to provide hyperlinked access to Web-accessible resources via library-maintained Web pages. Indeed one might consider Web pages maintained by library subject specialists to be an adjunct to the online catalog. Such pages may provide access to many resources previously not thought of as suitable for inclusion in the online catalog. In developing and maintaining such pages, government documents specialists and others must consider several relevant issues. Some thought must be given to the organizing principle to be used in constructing a set of links. A poorly organized set of links will be of little use to library patrons, and even a well thought out arrangement can be difficult to navigate without some sort of local search capability. Choices must be made as to whether to link to specific documents (and if so, how many of them) or to link to an agency's home page and let the user navigate to specific items from there. The latter approach will require less Web page development and maintenance, but will almost certainly result in increased reference work to assist users and/or less success by users in finding the information needed.

In the case of serials the feasibility of linking to the "current" issue of a given title may depend upon the publishing agency's practice in posting the material. Some agencies may post each issue with a specific file name (e.g., vol7_no2.html), which necessitates that the library trying to link to the current issue update its link as often as the title is published. A better alternative would be for current issues to have a consistent file name (e.g., current.html), with the file being renamed once a new issue has been released. Unfortunately, such practice is not the norm, so that library web authors must balance the desire to provide links to specific current data with the need to minimize time spent on Web page maintenance. This is a specific example of how the skill with which agency Web sites are designed can have a major impact on the amount of difficulty library web authors will have in providing access to official publications. Libraries seeking to provide anything even approaching a comprehensive set of links face a monumental task. More feasible for most libraries is a smaller, more focused set of links tailored to the users of a specific institution. Such a Web site is more along the lines of a ready reference collection than a full-scale digital library, and may be just what is called for to supplement the information available through the library catalog.

CONCLUSION

As can be seen from this discussion, the increasing reliance on electronic forms of dissemination for government serials presents libraries with a host of questions and challenges. In some cases, it has exacerbated preexisting problems in the distribution of government data, such as inconsistent patterns of publication, title changes and format changes. It also presents several new challenges in connecting users to the most current data in the online environment. Clearly, the fluidity of the medium calls for a flexible approach on the part of libraries to dealing with these many issues, as well as a high degree of awareness and sophistication about the characteristics of online information. Yet every challenge can also be seen as an opportunity. In this instance our opportunity is to increase access to a historically underutilized resource and provide its information content to library users in a format suitable to their needs. While the move to the electronic environment presents serious difficulties to overcome in the short run, ultimately perhaps it will allow us to at last include these valuable materials in the mainstream of library collections.

REFERENCES

1. Karen D. Darling, "Integrating Depository Documents Serials into Regular Serials Receiving and Cataloging Routines at the University of Oregon Library," *Advances in Serials Management* 5 (1995): 99-103.

2. Superintendent of Documents, "Format of Publications Distributed to Depository Libraries," *Administrative Notes* 8 (1987): 23.

3. Joe Morehead, "Lost and Gone Forever: The Demise of Selected Federal Serials," *The Serials Librarian* 12, No. 3/4 (1987): 6-7.

4. United States Congress. Joint Committee on Printing. *Provision of Federal Government Publications in Electronic Format to Depository Libraries: Report of the Ad Hoc Committee on Depository Library Access to Federal Automated Data Bases.* Washington: Government Printing Office, 1984, p. 10-11.

5. There are a number of examples of instances in which the use of electronic distribution methods has been mandated or encouraged by legislative action, notably in the *Legislative Branch Appropriations Acts* for 1996 (Public Law 104-53) and other appropriations bills.

6. United States. Government Printing Office. *Report to the Congress: Study to Identify Measures Necessary for a Successful Transition to a More Electronic Federal Depository Library Program.* Washington: Government Printing Office, June, 1996.

7. Claude Fleury and Yvon Bernatchez. *Distribution of Information: How to Select the Appropriate Technology.* Ottawa: Canada Communications Group, 1993.

8. Kristin D. Vogel, "Integrating Electronic Resources into Collection Development Policies," *Collection Management* 21, No. 2 (1996): 68.

9. Anthony W. Ferguson, "Interesting Problems Encountered on My Way to Writing an Electronic Information Collection Development Statement," *Against the Grain* 7 (April, 1995): 18.

10. Perhaps the best known producer of the type of service is the Congressional Information Service, Inc., which provides microfiche sets and indexing for various categories of government publications (e.g., statistical publications, reports to Congress, etc.).

11. United States. Superintendent of Documents. *Recommended Specifications for Public Access Work Stations in Federal Depository Libraries* (Available online: http://www.access.gpo.gov/su_docs/dpos/mintech.html).

A Survey of Standards for Identifying Serial Items on the Internet

Jennifer L. Marill

SUMMARY. This article explores current and proposed standards for identifying serial items on the Internet. Use of these standards will result in a library's ability to purchase individual electronic journal titles as well as component pieces (articles) and provide detailed catalog links to them. In addition, the standards could enable sophisticated copyright management systems. The standards discussed include the following: the Serial Item and Contribution Identifier, the Digital Object Identifier, the Publisher Item Identifier and the Internet standards, Uniform Resource Locator and Uniform Resource Name, for naming and describing networked resources on the World Wide Web. *[Article copies available for a fee from The Haworth Document Delivery Service: 1-800-342-9678. E-mail address: getinfo@haworthpressinc.com]*

INTRODUCTION

Currently in the world of library acquisitions and collection management there is much discussion about the selection of and access to electronic journals and articles. Publishers, serial vendors and other secondary source suppliers are offering a growing number of journal titles and packages for

---

Jennifer L. Marill is Systems Librarian for Technical Services and Collection Development, Washington Research Library Consortium, 901 Commerce Drive, Upper Marlboro, MD 20774.

[Haworth co-indexing entry note]: "A Survey of Standards for Identifying Serial Items on the Internet." Marill, Jennifer L. Co-published simultaneously in *The Acquisitions Librarian* (The Haworth Press, Inc.) No. 21, 1999, pp. 83-91; and: *Periodical Acquisitions and the Internet* (ed: Nancy Slight-Gibney) The Haworth Press, Inc., 1999, pp. 83-91. Single or multiple copies of this article are available for a fee from The Haworth Document Delivery Service [1-800-342-9678, 9:00 a.m. - 5:00 p.m. (EST). E-mail address: getinfo@haworthpressinc.com].

purchase to libraries and library consortia. Typically a prepackaged set of titles is sold to a library or consortium, and often some titles are included in these packages which an individual library has little interest in obtaining. Most institutions would prefer to have the option of purchasing individual titles or even selected articles within journals.

Why is it that more vendors and publishers are not providing access to their electronic journals at the title, article or other content level to libraries? Rather than explore the intellectual decision-making process for when to purchase packages of electronic titles versus component pieces, this article will focus on the standards and mechanisms that will enable a library to purchase these component pieces if they so desire. The standards or "item identification" mechanisms enabling this commerce are all available today, although some are in testing. It is important that acquisitions librarians are aware of these standards and encourage publishers and vendors to participate in the standards development process.

The following standards discussed here are typically known as unique item identifiers. The potential benefits of item identification are considerable. Chief among these benefits for acquisitions librarians is the ability to transact business with suppliers and track transactions between and among systems on the Internet. Potential byproducts of enhanced item tracking are new document delivery options. In addition, library catalog links can be made directly from online citations to the electronic articles, even linking from citation to citation across databases and other networked resources. Users can be informed of copyright ownership and the terms and conditions of access. Copyright owners gain the facility to collect and distribute fees, and therefore are more willing to give permission for the use of their electronic materials.[1] Libraries can track what items are being used and thus manage their collections more efficiently. In our rapidly growing electronic environment the ability to uniquely label or identify every item of information will become more and more critical.

THE SERIAL ITEM AND CONTRIBUTION IDENTIFIER (SICI)

The original version of the SICI standard was approved by NISO (National Information Standards Organization) in 1991 and known as the ANSI/NISO Z39.56 standard. The standard defines the requirements for constructing a variable length code that provides unique identification of serial items (issues of journals) and contributions (articles) contained in them. The standard is intended to be used primarily by the bibliographic community and those involved in the use or management of serial titles and their contributions.[2] The standard was recently revised in 1996 to accommodate the growth of online abstracting and indexing (A & I) and document delivery services interested in using the standard for rights management and electronic document identification on the Internet. Many acquisitions librarians are familiar with the machine-readable SICI barcode, which many publishers are now printing on their serial publications. Major library system vendors and subscription agents have developed interfaces for these barcodes for use in automated check-in systems.

The 1991 version of the SICI established two levels of coding: a unique code for the identification of an issue of a serial title called the Serial Item Identifier, and a unique code for individual contributions within a serial, called the Serial Contribution Identifier. The 1996 revision included a number of changes facilitating its use in EDI (Electronic Data Interchange) transactions and the linking of an original work, a citation and A & I databases in a networked environment. The revision now establishes the SICI code as a sequence of defined segments: item, contribution and control. Systems and applications will now be better able to parse and process specific segments and their data elements. Thus, the 1996 version has a greater potential for item identification than the original 1991 version. As reported by Julia Blixrud in *SISAC News*[3] the major changes to the standard are as follows:

- A Code Structure Identifier (CSI) specifies the data elements that are present in the segments of the SICI. Three CSIs were defined in version 2: CSI-1 identifies a serial item (journal issue), CSI-2 specifies a contribution (article) within a serial item, and CSI-3 identifies locally assigned contribution identifiers.
- A method was established to indicate the medium used for distribution of serial items. The standard allows users to tell whether the item or contribution being identified is paper, microform, electronic, etc.
- The standard now provides for the coding of a derivative part of a serial item or contribution, including tables of contents, indexes or abstracts. A mechanism is also established to allow other codes for identifiable derivative parts (e.g., charts, graphs, tables) to be developed and incorporated into the standard.
- The Title Code was expanded to assure the probability of uniqueness for contribution identification.

The SICI code is consistent with other standards that address serials, such as the International Standard Serial Number (ISSN) used to identify a serial title. In order for a SICI to be assigned, a serial title must have been assigned an ISSN. The use of ISSNs has proved invaluable for identifying and linking to serial titles. Active members of the serials standards community are convinced that use of the SICI will prove just as beneficial for identification and commercial transactions of serial components. An example of a SICI for the article: Blixrud, Julia C. "ISSN in the CONSER Database," *CONSER*, no. 19

(June 1990), pp. 6-7 would appear as: 0163-8610(199006)19<6.IITCD>2.0.TX;2-L.

DIGITAL OBJECT IDENTIFIER (DOI)

The DOI is being developed by the Association of American Publishers (AAP), in partnership with the Corporation for National Research Initiatives (CNRI) and R. R. Bowker, a division of Reed Elsevier, Inc. The DOI is a system for identifying digital objects in order to facilitate electronic commerce and copyright management. The DOI is described as "the license plate for digital content on the information superhighway,"[4] which will provide a unique and persistent identifier for electronic information resources.

The Bowker/CNRI team has focused on three key areas during the first year of development: developing a numbering system for identifying digital objects created by publishers; creating an agency for assigning publisher numbers; and developing a network-based directory to link digital objects to their publisher.[5] DOIs could be assigned to any electronic object that is likely to be individually bought, sold and electronically downloaded or retrieved. Once a DOI is assigned to an object it is never reassigned, and there is no limit to the number or size of objects that can be identified by a DOI. A DOI may be assigned to complex works such as an encyclopedia, or to individual chapters, tables, or even photographs. In the music publishing industry, a DOI might identify recordings, videos or other creative works–tremendously enlarging the universe of copyrighted, salable objects.[6]

The DOI is a two-part identifier, separated by a slash, as in 10.1048/872. The first part of the number to the left of the slash is a registrant's prefix, assigned by a DOI agency. The prefix (10.1048) consists of the numbering agency and publisher. To the right of the slash is a publisher-chosen identifier that can be either a random number or any other internal numbering system that a publisher uses (examples include a SICI or Publisher Item Identifier [PII], chronological numbering, sequential numbering, etc.). The number, however, should be unique to that publisher. Assignment of DOIs can be automated and done in the course of normal publishing operations.

A DOI agency is a central organization responsible for maintaining the DOI directory and ensuring the integrity of the system. When users search the DOI directory with a WWW browser, the directory links the permanently assigned DOI to the URL containing the desired object. The directory is a distributed computer system publicly accessible across the Internet. When a change of copyright ownership occurs, the DOI remains the same but a new pointer (associated address) is entered in the directory to ensure persistence.

Additional information about the DOI can be obtained from the DOI homepage, www.doi.org. A working prototype was unveiled at the Frankfurt

Book Fair in October 1997. A subsequent press release stated that the DOI system, presented to a standing room only audience of international publishers, was a hit. The DOI presentation also resulted in the establishment of the new Internal Digital Object Identifier Foundation, which will administer the DOI system.[7]

PUBLISHER ITEM IDENTIFIER (PII)

The Publisher Item Identifier (PII) is an internal numbering system developed by scientific, technical and medical (STM) publishers and primarily used for prepublication control. Agreed upon in 1995, publishers sought to create an identifier that uniquely identifies a document. The goal was to create an identifier that is format independent; easy to generate and use; capable of describing different manifestations of the same document; generated by the originator of the published item (i.e., the publisher) prior to actual publication; and compatible with existing related standards.

The PII is a string of 17 alphanumeric characters: S0165-3806(96)00403-8.[8] The first element indicates the source publication type, e.g., "S" for serials, "B" for books. The second element is the publication identifier, ISSN or ISBN. The third element in parentheses is the year of assignment, a mandatory element for serials. The fourth element is an item number assigned by the publisher. The last element is a one-character check digit. The ISBN and ISSN are used as part of the number but only to ensure uniqueness, as the PII itself is considered a "dumb" number. The PII can only be assigned and maintained by the publisher.

Norman Paskin, in his article on information identifiers, notes that publishers have been criticized for using the PII because of its reliance on a publication identifier designed for printed items, namely, the ISSN. In the future documents may not be grouped in such a way that an assignment of an ISSN is valid. However, STM publishers, while recognizing this limitation, wanted to use an existing standard in a system that could be implemented now. The PII does allow extension to component identification (e.g., table, abstract, etc.), but there is no detailed specification for this presently.[9] Green and Bide state that "although the PII is well designed to track publication items throughout their life cycle, it is unsuitable for use in ordering or claims transactions, requests for permissions or as an aid to finding published articles."[10]

INTERNET NAMES AND ADDRESSES

The Uniform Resource Locator (URL) and Uniform Resource Name (URN) comprise the structure for naming and describing networked resources on the World Wide Web (WWW). The URL describes specific locations or addresses for documents rather than describing the documents themselves. The URL is now a stable and standard technology, but often subject to change when hardware and file systems are reorganized. To assure persistence of URLs, two methods of naming have been proposed: the Corporation for National Research Initiatives HANDLE System and the OCLC Persistent Uniform Resource Locator (PURL) system. Instead of pointing directly to an Internet location, a PURL points to an intermediate resolution service that maintains a database linking the PURL to its current URL and returning that URL to the user. When a URL changes, the associated PURL only needs to be changed once on the PURL server, as long as the resolution service continues to operate. OCLC is now freely distributing the PURL source code in order to promote its widespread use.

The URN is being developed to assign persistent, unique, location-independent identifiers to Internet resources. There is interest in having a specific URN always associated with the same resource, although it is not clear yet how URNs will be mapped to individual resources. The assignment of names could be designated to naming authorities, which would define criteria for determining when new names are assigned.[11] A central registry has been proposed as a vehicle for coordination among naming authorities. In any event, it has been acknowledged that the URN must support existing naming schemes, such as the PII and SICI.

CONCLUSION

Presently there is no single, accepted standard for uniquely identifying electronic documents. There has been concern about the proliferation of identifier systems, but there has also been much cooperation among various organizations in the last few years. The Serials Industry Systems Advisory Committee (SISAC) is one such organization actively bringing together the many players in the serials world and providing a forum for discussion and cooperation. Efforts are also being made to ensure that the various standards coexist rather than compete with each other. For example, the DOI numbering syntax is consistent with Internet standards activities in that it complies with the syntax for a URN. AAP is working closely with other industry identifier systems to ensure cross-industry compatibility. It is still not clear how the DOI would relate to the SICI and other identification schemes. The scope of the proposed DOI is wider (intellectual property rights), but it is also acknowledged that a key aim of the DOI system is the ability to link to other systems (ISSN, PII, SICI, URL, etc.) and become an integrating "lingua franca" service.[12] The DOI has been particularly beneficial to the SICI community because it has become clear that SICIs are the best tools for identifying content within the DOI. In DOI testing, those who already had SICIs were able to move much more quickly than those participants who were trying to figure out some sort of internal identifier.[13]

The PII and SICI version 2 attempt to meet different needs, but they are compatible and in some cases complementary. A SICI may be assigned retrospectively, and is primarily an aid to finding existing published articles or issues. The PII is assigned exclusively by the publisher and only on items 1996 and later. The revised SICI's three Code Structures (CSI) allow for reference to other forms of identification called "locally assigned identifiers," which include the PII. A publisher may use both the SICI version 2 and PII (either separately or combined in CSI-3 format) in his published materials, depending upon the required function and recipient. It is also important to remember that a PII can be applied to book contributions, whereas a SICI is restricted to serials.[14]

It is obvious from this brief summary of standards that there are still many issues to be worked out. The standards here represent efforts towards creating unique identifiers, but it remains to be seen whether publishers, intermediary aggregators, librarians and others in the serials information chain will adopt and actively use unique identifiers for electronic commerce, enhanced document delivery and increased database linkage. Identifiers serve multiple purposes, and it may not be possible for one identifier to satisfy the needs of all involved communities. Norman Paskin in his article, "Information Identifiers," brings up the issue of the "versions" problem, which may cause acquisitions librarians the biggest headache. The treatment of different versions of an electronic resource has not been addressed in most identifier discussions. In the world of printed journals, a separate ISSN is typically assigned to another edition of the same journal. This difference is often murkier in the world of electronic materials. Paskin states, "For some purposes, such as ordering, we may need to distinguish versions which are intellectually identical even if physically distinct, and this must be a capability of the overall identification mechanism."[15] Identifiers will need to be flexible and expandable, as we do not yet know their role in a more fully commercial electronic world.

REFERENCES

1. Anne Ramsden, "Copyright Management Technologies," Ariadne (The Web Version), Issue 10 (July 1997). Available from: *http://www.ariadne.ac.uk/issue10/copyright*.

2. ANSI/NISO Z39.56-1996 Version 2, *http://sunsite.berkeley.edu/SICI*.

3. Julia C. Blixrud, "Version 2 of SICI Published," *SISAC News* 11, No. 2 (Winter 1996/Spring 1997): 9-10.

4. "AAP Unveils DOI at PSP Confab: Publisher Interested but Wary," *Publishers Weekly* 244, No. 8 (February 24, 1997): 11.
5. "Team Selected to Develop Digital Object Identifier System for Publishing Industry," A Press Release from the Association of American Publishers (AAP), Washington, DC, September 9, 1996 as reprinted in *SISAC News* 12, No. 1 (Summer/Fall 1997): 15-17.
6. The Digital Object Identifier System, *http://www.doi.org*.
7. Association of American Publishers, *AAAP News,* October 16, 1997. Available from: *http://www.publishers.org/news/releases/frankfurt.html*.
8. "Publisher Item Identifier as a means of document identification." Available from: *http://www.elsevier.nl/inca/homepage/about/pii*.
9. "Publisher Item Identifier as a means of document identification." Available from: *http://www.elsevier.nl/inca/homepage/about/pii*.
10. Brian Green and Mark Bide, "Unique Identifiers: A Brief Introduction." Available from: *http://www.bic.org.uk/bic/uniquid.html*.
11. Jennifer A. Younger, "Resources Description in the Digital Age," *Library Trends* 45, No. 3 (Winter 1997), p. 483.
12. Norman Paskin, "Information Identifiers." (1997). Available from: *http://www/elsevier.nl/inca/homepage/about/infoident*.
13. Private email from Julia Blixrud.
14. Norman Paskin, "Information Identifiers." (1997). Available from: *http://www/elsevier.nl/inca/homepage/about/infoident*.
15. Norman Paskin, "Information Identifiers." (1997). Available from: *http://www/elsevier.nl/inca/homepage/about/infoident*.

BIBLIOGRAPHY

"AAP Unveils DOI at PSP Confab: Publisher Interested but Wary." *Publishers Weekly* 244, No. 8 (February 24, 1997): 11.
Blixrud, Julia C., "Version 2 of SICI Published," *SISAC News* 11, No. 2 (Winter 1996/Spring 1997): 9-10.
DOI homepage: *http://www.doi.org*.
Duranceau, Ellen Finnie, column editor of The Balance Point, "Naming and Describing Networked Electronic Resources: The Role of Uniform Resource Identifiers." *Serials Review* 20, No. 4 (Winter 1994): 31-44.
Green, Brian and Bide, Mark. (1997). "Unique Identifiers: A Brief Introduction." Available from: *http://www.bic.org.uk/bic/uniquid.html*.
Lynch, Clifford A., "Building the Infrastructure of Resource Sharing: Union Catalogs, Distributed Search, and Cross-Database Linkage," *Library Trends* 45, No. 3 (Winter 1997): 448-461.
Lynch, Clifford, "Technology and its Implication for Serials Acquisition," *Against the Grain* 9, No. 1 (February 1997): 34-37.
Needleman, Mark H. "Standards for the Global Information Infrastructure," *Information Standards Quarterly* 8, No. 2 (April 1996): 1-5.
Nye, Julie Blume, " Integrating Serials into the Triangle Research Libraries Network Document Delivery System," *The Serials Librarian* 31, No. 3 (1997): 29-48.

Paskin, Norman. (1997). "Information Identifiers." Available from: *http://www/elsevier.nl/inca/homepage/about/infoident*.

"Publisher Item Identifier as a means of document identification." Available from: *http://www.elsevier.nl/inca/homepage/about/pii*.

Ramsden, Anne, "Copyright Management Technologies," Ariadne (The Web Version), Issue 10 (July 1997). Available from: *http://www.ariadne.ac.uk/issue10/copyright*.

Risher, Carol, "The Digital Object Identifier–A Tool for Online Commerce," *SISAC News* 12, No. 1 (Summer/Fall): 10-12.

Simmonds, Albert, "Standard Identifiers in the Electronic Age," *SISAC News* 12, No. 1 (Summer/Fall 1997): 8-10.

SICI Version 2 standard: (1997). Available from: *http://sunsite.berkeley.edu/SICI*.

SISAC homepage: *http://www.bookwire.com/bisg/sisac.html#membership*.

"Team Selected to Develop Digital Object Identifier System for Publishing Industry," A Press Release from the Association of American Publishers (AAP), Washington, DC, September 9, 1996 as reprinted in *SISAC News* 12, No. 1 (Summer/Fall 1997): 15-17.

Weston, Beth and Blixrud, Julia C., "Report of the SISAC General Meeting, 'Digital Article Identifiers and Rights Management,' " *SISAC News* 12, No. 1 (Summer/Fall 1997): 5-8.

Younger, Jennifer A., "Resources Description in the Digital Age," *Library Trends* 45, No. 3 (Winter 1997): 462-487.

The Internet:
An Essential Tool
for Law Library Serials Acquisitions

Marla J. Schwartz
Susan J. Kimball

SUMMARY. The World Wide Web has transformed the way acquisitions and serials departments do business. Internet transactions have become integral to our work. This article describes how the Acquisitions and Serials Department at the Washington College of Law Library has integrated the Internet into daily workflow, using e-mail, FTP, and the World Wide Web. Practical applications of each are described. Specific library, publisher, and vendor Web sites that are particularly useful for law libraries are illustrated. *[Article copies available for a fee from The Haworth Document Delivery Service: 1-800-342-9678. E-mail address: getinfo@haworthpressinc.com]*

INTRODUCTION

Early articles about using the Internet in library technical services seem to have been written to justify and encourage its use, emphasizing that the Internet was not just for reference or research.[1] In 1995, Marylou Hale traced

---

Marla J. Schwartz is Chief, Acquisitions and Serials Department (e-mail: mschwar@wcl.american.edu), and Susan J. Kimball is Serials and Technical Systems Coordinator (e-mail: skimbal@wcl.american.edu), both at the Washington College of Law Library, American University, 4801 Massachusetts Avenue, NW, Washington, DC 20016-8182.

[Haworth co-indexing entry note]: "The Internet: An Essential Tool for Law Library Serials Acquisitions." Schwartz, Marla J., and Susan J. Kimball. Co-published simultaneously in *The Acquisitions Librarian* (The Haworth Press, Inc.) No. 21, 1999, pp. 93-103; and: *Periodical Acquisitions and the Internet* (ed: Nancy Slight-Gibney) The Haworth Press, Inc., 1999, pp. 93-103. Single or multiple copies of this article are available for a fee from The Haworth Document Delivery Service [1-800-342-9678, 9:00 a.m. - 5:00 p.m. (EST). E-mail address: getinfo@haworthpressinc.com].

© 1999 by The Haworth Press, Inc. All rights reserved.

the history of the Internet and discussed the changes its use brought to acquisitions activities at the University of Nevada, Las Vegas.[2] By using e-mail, FTP, and remote login, librarians and staff were able to create new workflow models incorporating these technologies and streamlining the acquisitions process. That same year, Jack Montgomery addressed use of the Internet in an academic law library, specifically, listservs, FTP, and telnet access to vendors' databases.[3] In the last two years, Internet use in libraries has skyrocketed with the ease of use of the World Wide Web. In the Acquisitions and Serials Department at American University's Washington College of Law Library we use the Internet, particularly the World Wide Web, in every activity from selecting to replacing serials.

All librarians and full-time staff at the WCL Library have workstations with ready access to the Internet via e-mail and the World Wide Web, and the library's integrated online system, INNOPAC. Our most heavily-used patron workstations provide access to the library's home page (http://library.wcl.american.edu) and the Web version of the catalog (http://leagle.wcl.american.edu/screens/opacmenu.html). Here patrons find links to many other Web-based library catalogs as well as popular research tools such as *THOMAS* from the Library of Congress and *Congressional Universe* from the Congressional Information Service, Inc. Our catalog also provides either a telnet or Web interface to the *Legal Resource Index*. Telnet access to other law libraries, our main library, and the Library of Congress is available from our character-based OPAC, in-house and remotely for those affiliated with American University.

The WCL Library and the law libraries of Georgetown University and George Washington University were the first INNOPAC libraries to link our catalogs by dial-in access using modems, later replaced by telnet and now Web access. Reference librarians and our users have long been accustomed to checking other local library catalogs for items we do not own. Acquisitions and Serials staff routinely check other catalogs for items requested for ordering and to see if missing serial issues have been received by other libraries.

E-MAIL, LISTSERVS, AND FTP

As in most libraries, e-mail was probably our first introduction to the Internet. Now e-mail has become the primary means of communicating within the library, with law school faculty, and with vendors and publishers. It eliminates the need to leave phone messages and facilitates easy responses, especially from busy faculty with irregular work schedules, and establishes a written record of the transaction. E-mail is especially useful for contacting overseas vendors because it eliminates the problems associated with different time zones. We send order inquiries, orders, claims, and cancellations by e-mail. We create lists using the INNOPAC system, reformat them, and e-mail them directly from the system to the vendor. Although we do not have the electronic ordering module of INNOPAC, this procedure works in a similar way.

E-mail listservs have opened the lines of communication among those involved in serials acquisitions. Members of the Acquisitions and Serials Department subscribe to SERIALST[4] and ACQNET,[5] which discuss a variety of topics related to serials management and acquisitions from specific journal questions to association meeting announcements. Several of us also subscribe to the INNOPAC[6] discussion list, which provides a forum for discussion of system-related issues. There are also two listservs that are useful specifically for law library acquisitions: LAWACQ,[7] a distribution list of law acquisitions librarians maintained by Cynthia Aninao at the University of Cincinnati Law Library and the NEWLAWBOOKS-L[8] list maintained by Mark Folmsbee at Washburn University Law Library. LAWACQ was created because many law acquisitions librarians wanted a forum more specific than the general LAW-LIB[9] list to discuss issues unique to acquisitions. NEW-LAWBOOKS-L is used heavily by legal publishers to announce their new publications and we forward these announcements to library faculty for collection development decisions. Our primary vendor for legal periodicals, William S. Hein & Co., Inc., maintains a listerv called HEIN-SUBS-L[10] on which they post up-to-date information about delayed issues, title changes, cessations, and the like. This list is extremely useful in day-to-day serials work. NEWJOUR,[11] maintained by Ann Okerson and James J. O'Donnell, announces new electronic journals and is useful for collection development.

More sophisticated than moderated listservs, electronic newsletters have also become valuable in serials acquisitions work. We receive the *Newsletter on Serials Pricing Issues*,[12] one of the first electronic newsletters to foster discussion about the increasing costs of serials, and forward it to our head of collection development. The full text of all issues of the *Newsletter* from its inception in 1989 is archived (http://www.lib.unc.edu/prices/). The Technical Services Special Interest Section of the American Association of Law Libraries (AALL) publishes the *Technical Services Law Librarian* and makes the latest issue and some back issues available on its home page (http://www.aallnet.org/sis/tssis/tsll/tsll.htm). This newsletter, also available in print as part of membership in the section, contains a serials column which tracks title changes and cessations, as well as an acquisitions column with useful information on the volatile world of legal publishing. The Committee on Relations with Information Vendors (CRIV) of AALL also has a Web site where it posts up-to-date information about the resolution of complaints against legal publishers and vendors (http://www.aallnet.org/committee/criv/).

We also use file transfer protocol (FTP) to obtain electronic publications.

Our faculty make extensive use of a publication produced weekly by the University of Washington Law Library called *Current Index to Legal Periodicals (CILP)*. We obtain it every week using FTP from one of our PCs and then send it to the faculty as an attachment to an e-mail message. Alternatively, faculty can create their own profiles using the University of Washington Web site, allowing them to receive individually customized issues by e-mail each week without intervention by the library. This method has saved us the over $3000 cost of paper issues for each faculty member, as well as the cost of check-in and processing of individual issues. To request photocopies of articles, faculty can cut and paste the citations into an e-mail message to our Interlibrary Loan staff. In the near future, we hope to make the *CILP* available for the WCL community on our Web site.

Perhaps our most sophisticated use of the Internet is in the area of file transfer for invoice processing. While it is not true Electronic Data Interchange (EDI) in the sense of machine-to-machine transactions without human intervention, it is truly a time and labor-saving innovation. We use INNOPAC's file transfer software to obtain invoices from two of our periodical vendors. They notify us by e-mail when an invoice is available for FTP, and we access their systems to download it. INNOPAC gets the invoice and stores it in a file to be reviewed by our accounts specialist who either approves or rejects the charges. Once a charge is accepted, payment information is posted to individual serial order records. This frees her from the tedious job of manually posting payments for many serial titles. We continue to receive a paper copy of the invoice from the vendor because of our Controller's Office requirements. File transfer can also be used to send lists of orders, claims, or transfers from the INNOPAC to serials vendors.[13]

THE WORLD WIDE WEB

The World Wide Web has transformed serials acquisitions operations in libraries, and law libraries are no exception.[14] Several Web sites have been developed that aid in identifying the abundant resources that exist on the Internet. *AcqWeb*, created and maintained by Anna Belle Leiserson at Vanderbilt University Law Library, is well-known to most acquisitions librarians (http://www.library.vanderbilt.edu/law/acqs/acqs.html). We use it to locate e-mail addresses and URLs for vendors' and publishers' Web sites, many of which we use extensively. Another site that identifies resources is the *Top 200 Technical Services Benefits of Home Page Development* (http://tpot.ucsd.edu/cataloging/misc/top200.html) maintained by Barbara Stewart as part of the *Technical Processing Online Tools (TPOT)* home page (http://tpot.ucsd.edu/).[15] *LIBLICENSE: Licensing Digital Information* (http://www.library.yale.edu/~llicense/index.shtml) has become increasingly useful in helping us sort out the array of licensing agreements that accompany new electronic resources. It includes sample publishers' licenses, a licensing vocabulary, and the archives of the LIBLICENSE-L discussion list.[16]

Most academic law libraries and many law firms have ready access to the Web and many of them also maintain home pages. Several of the larger academic law libraries have created their own home pages with useful information for library users and staff. The Lillian Goldman Law Library at Yale University has developed a Technical Services home page which includes links to many of the legal publishers and vendors that we will describe here (http://elsinore.cis.yale.edu/lawweb/tech.htm). The Law Library at the University of Virginia provides similar links on the Librarians' Pages section of its home page which can be found under Internet Resources (http://www.law.virginia.edu/Libitc.htm). Georgetown University's E. B. Williams Law Library Technical Services home page also provides links to publishers and vendors as well as law and library-related organizations and electronic publications (http://www.ll.georgetown.edu:80/tchsrv/techserv.html). Some technical services departments have also posted library procedures on their Web sites. An excellent example is the University of Colorado Law Library Technical Services Home Page (http://www.colorado.edu/law/lawlib/ts/index.html) which includes procedures and tools for acquisitions and cataloging, as well as links to publisher and vendor contacts. The home page of the University of Washington Libraries Acquisitions Division (http://weber.u.washington.edu/~acqdiv/) also includes department procedures. Peter Stevens, the developer of this site, has divided it into information for selectors and acquisitions staff and includes a rated list of links to other acquisitions departments' Web sites.[17]

Increasingly, law libraries have made their catalogs accessible via the Web, eliminating the need for complicated telnet connections and terminal emulation software. Searching other catalogs allows us to confirm receipt dates of serial issues as a routine step in the claiming process, thus avoiding premature claims. We also use other catalogs as a resource to confirm bibliographic information and publication status of items requested by faculty and students.

PUBLISHERS' WEB SITES

In addition to the proliferation of library catalogs on the Web, vendors and publishers have established a major presence there, providing a wealth of information for serials acquisitions. Subscription agents and publishers of legal materials have home pages of varying qualities, many of which have greatly facilitated the ordering and claiming process. The sites offer a variety of services from online ordering and claiming to catalog searching and bibliographic verification. In this section, we will describe some of the primary legal publisher sites and a few other pages that we find useful and have incorporated into our daily workflow. As with most of the World Wide Web, these sites are constantly being revised and updated.

The American Bar Association (http://www.abanet.org/) site is useful for checking what publications are available for purchase as well as ordering online. The complete catalog is keyword searchable as well as browsable alphabetically, by subject, or by broad categories, e.g., materials for and about bar associations, professional books, and periodicals. The page also advertises new publications for collection development purposes. You can either order materials online securely with a credit card or submit the order online and request that a customer service representative contact you to obtain billing information.

A second legal publisher that maintains a Web presence is the Bureau of National Affairs (http://www.bna.com). The BNA site facilitates address changes and replacement ordering by offering online forms that eliminate the need for excessive phone calls and letter writing. Contact information for a variety of services is also provided in order to facilitate communicating your needs to the appropriate department at BNA. In addition, there are links to all of the various BNA subsidiaries' Web sites (e.g., Tax Management, Inc., BNA Books, and Pike & Fischer, Inc.) which vary greatly in quality and content. The site is relatively difficult to navigate, however, because of inconsistent navigation tools and bad links.

BNA also provides a special service called BNA PLUS that provides information through the Web site. "[It] is a division of BNA's editorial department. BNA PLUS provides customer support and specialized information assistance, including research and document retrieval, that complements and supplements BNA subscription publications and services."[18] The information on the Web site includes CD-ROM and electronic publishing technical support and detailed information on document delivery and custom research services.

BNA also offers a complete product catalog that provides access by general subject area, format (what BNA calls delivery mode), or alphabetically. There is also a feature called "Quick Products Viewer" that allows you to designate the topic and delivery mode in order to limit retrieval to only those products that fit the criteria. The button for this feature, however, is difficult to find as it appears only at the bottom of the alphabetical listings and not on any of the initial product catalog screens. The entries for each title are limited to a brief description about the product and do not include any pricing information.

Another site is the Commerce Clearing House, Inc. home page (http://www.cch.com/). CCH provides an extremely efficient method of ordering replacement pages and reports, saving time for the library staff and CCH customer service representatives who no longer must make telephone contact. Most items ordered online are received within a week. Also available on the home page are FAQs and contact information for ordering, as well as links to a variety of CCH affiliates both domestic and international. The site is completely searchable which facilitates locating specific information quickly.

The Matthew Bender Site (http://www.bender.com/) is similar to the other legal sites in its offerings. It has a searchable bookstore which is essentially a product catalog including Matthew Bender and Shepard's CD-ROMs and print products. If you register on the Bender site you can fill a virtual shopping cart with products and order them online. The Shepard's Citations section of the Web site allows for fee-based searching of the entire Shepard's Citation collection or by any of the states or regions corresponding to the print publications. Payment is made by credit card over a secure network.

The Lexis Law Publishing site (http://www.lexislawpublishing.com) provides an extensive product catalog that is arranged in a variety of ways. A clickable imagemap of the United States provides access to state materials and lists links to official state home pages. All products can be browsed by title or searched by topic, jurisdiction, keyword, author, or ISBN. New publications are highlighted on the site as well as some full-text products which are provided at no charge. Contact information is provided for customer service, technical support, and individual authors using Lexis as a liaison. Lexis Law Publishing incorporates the Michie Company and Butterworth Legal Publishing.

The Research Institute of America (RIA) Web site (http://www.riatax.com) provides a variety of current news items in addition to its publication information. It updates its Weekly News section regularly. The product catalog on the RIA site includes information on CD-ROM and print publications. It is not searchable and prices are not available for all titles. There are, however, some brochures and demonstrations of products available for viewing. RIA can be contacted for address changes, replacement pages, and other inquiries through the RIA Group customer service page (http://www.riag.com/cs.htm).

Warren, Gorham & Lamont, a division of the RIA Group, has a limited Web site (http://www.wgl.com). It provides access to the complete catalog which is arranged topically and alphabetically within each topic. It is not searchable but does include an extensive price list. The best feature of the WG&L site is the ability to order products online using a valid account number so that no credit card transactions are required. Online customer service for WG&L is handled by the RIA Group (http://www.riag.com/cs.htm).

West Group, which at this time includes Bancroft-Whitney, Clark Boardman Callaghan, Lawyers Cooperative Publishing, Westlaw, and West Publishing, has developed a site that integrates all of the formerly independent company sites (http://www.westgroup.com/). Any of the old URLs will lead to the new West Group home page. The online product catalog is searchable by subject, jurisdiction, keyword, or title. Information about individual products varies depending on the original publisher; some provide only a simple description of the content while others supply the table of contents. Products can be ordered using a West account number or a credit card.

The World Wide Web has made it easier to keep track of the rapidly changing world of legal publishing. Rob Richards at the University of Colorado Law Library maintains *A Legal Publishers' List: The Shape of Legal Publishing Today* (http://www.colorado.edu/law/lawlib/ts/legpub.htm). The "list of corporate affiliations represents a collaborative effort by many librarians and legal information industry professionals on the LAW-LIB listserv to trace the current lines of ownership in the U.S. legal publishing industry."[19]

VENDORS' WEB SITES

Most of the major periodicals vendors have well-developed Web sites including such information as company history, contacts, product catalogs, and subscription price projections. We use Blackwell's Information Services for many of our non-legal periodicals. Blackwell's has consolidated the home pages of its components, formerly B. H. Blackwell's and Readmore, into one Web site (http://www.blackwell.co.uk/journals/). We find their Serials CONNECT service (http://eservices.blackwell.co.uk/serialconnect/) to be the most useful area of the Web site. This searchable database provides access to bibliographic and subscription information for more than 250,000 serials and series titles. Some of the entries include dispatch data for individual issues, as well as links to the publisher's Web site. CONNECT offers registered customers the added convenience of online ordering, claiming, and renewing. Blackwell's also offers useful links to electronic journals and newsletters, ILS vendors, library catalogs, and library-related organizations on its Web site (http://www.blackwell.co.uk/journals/info/index.html).

The William S. Hein & Co., Inc. site (http://lawlib.wuacc.edu/hein) has only a few useful features from the subscription department. You can search the current year archives of the HEIN-SUBS-L listserv which provides information on publishing status of many journals. Since Hein is the repository for back issues of most American law reviews, one of the most valuable features of the site is the master checklist for back issue prices and availability, which facilitates the ordering of replacement issues. The entries may be browsed alphabetically or searched by title keyword. Online ordering is offered for libraries that have a current account with Hein.

UMI, the major microforms vendor, now offers its *Serials in Microform* catalog on the Web (http://wwwlib.umi.com/sim/). It is searchable by title, subject, and commercial index. Prices for the various microform formats are provided as well as the ability to generate orders or price quotes for multiple volumes.

Our primary book vendor for non-legal publications is Yankee Book Peddler and we also purchase some standing orders through them. Their Web site (http://www.ybp.com) is extremely useful. We use GOBI, their bibliographic database available by password for customers, on a daily basis for searching and ordering. The continuations database can be searched separately, listing individual volumes and the library's receipt history. Orders can be placed through GOBI with the capability of linking to the INNOPAC for automatic creation of bibliographic and order records, another use of file transfer that has significantly altered the way libraries do business.[20]

In addition to publisher and vendor sites, the Web provides other useful resources for serials acquisitions. Xenon Laboratories maintains an easy to use currency converter (http://www.xe.net/currency/). United Parcel Service (http://www.ups.com) and Federal Express (http://www.fedex.com) provide the ability to track packages. Returns and other deliveries can be traced online using the tracking number assigned to every shipment.

CONCLUSION

The ease of use of the Web has drastically changed the daily workflow of serials acquisitions. Just as most of our students cannot remember a library with only a card catalog, most of us take for granted the ability to look at other library catalogs with the click of a mouse or contact our vendors without leaving phone messages and waiting days to be called back. Instead of reaching for the phone to get information on new publications and prices or find out if another library subscribes to a requested publication, we turn to the Internet. But as the Web has made our work faster and more efficient, it has also created demands that we sometimes cannot meet. Many legal serials are produced by smaller publishers who have not established a Web presence and/or still require a check with the order. In these cases, even the fax machine cannot speed up the process. As Virginia Scheschy has observed, publisher competition is fierce to create attractive and informative Web sites to appeal to potential library customers.[21] It has become apparent that those publishers and venders who wish to survive and increase their business will eventually be forced to use the Internet. No one can predict how it will evolve beyond the World Wide Web, but we are certain that the Internet will continue to be an essential tool for acquisitions in all types of libraries.

REFERENCES

1. See the following: Jeanne M.K. Boydston, "Serials Sources on the Web," *Serials Librarian* 29, no. 3/4 (1996): 175-187; Gillian M. McCombs, "The Internet and Technical Services: A Point Break Approach," *Library Resources & Technical Services* 38, no. 2 (April 1994): 169-177; Patricia Sayre McCoy, "Technical Services and the Internet," *Wilson Library Bulletin* 69 (March 1995): 37-40; Lauren Noel, "What's in It for Us?: Internet Use in Technical Services," *Serials Librarian* 28, no. 3/4 (1996): 317-323; Vicky Reich et al., "Electronic Discussion Lists and Journals: A Guide for Technical Services Staff," *Library Resources & Technical Services* 39, no. 3 (July 1995): 303-319.
2. Marylou Hale, "Automated Library Acquisitions: A New Model for Business," *The Acquisitions Librarian* 13/14 (1995): 65-82.
3. Jack Montgomery, "The Internet in Acquisitions Work: A Status Report," *Trends in Law Library Management and Technology* 6, no. 6 (Feb. 1995): 2-5.
4. To subscribe to SERIALST, send a message to listserv@list.uvm.edu that reads: SUBSCRIBE SERIALST Firstname Lastname. The archives can be found at http://list.uvm.edu/archives/serialst.html.
5. To subscribe to ACQNET, send a message to listserv@listserv.appstate.edu that reads: SUBSCRIBE ACQNET-L Firstname Lastname. The archives can be found at http://www.lib.ncsu.edu/stacks/a/acqnet/.
6. To subscribe to the INNOPAC listserv, send a message to listserv@maine.maine.edu that reads: SUBSCRIBE INNOPAC Firstname Lastname. The archives can be found at http://corso.ccsu.ctstateu.edu/~iii/1998/.
7. To subscribe to LAWACQ, send a message to cynthia.aninao@law.uc.edu.
8. To subscribe to NEWLAWBOOKS-L, send a message to listserv@lawlib.wuacc.edu that reads: SUBSCRIBE NEWLAWBOOKS-L. The archives can be found at http://www.findmail.com/listsaver/newlawbooks-l/.
9. To subscribe to LAW-LIB, send a message to listproc@ucdavis.edu that reads: SUBSCRIBE LAW-LIB. The archives can be found at http://www.findmail.com/listsaver/law-lib/.
10. To subscribe to the HEIN-SUBS-L listserv, send a message to listserv@lawlib.wuacc.edu that reads: SUBSCRIBE HEIN-SUBS-L. The archives can be found at http://ftplaw.wuacc.edu/listproc/hein-subs-l/.
11. To subscribe to NEWJOUR, complete the online form at http://gort.ucsd.edu/newjour/subscribe.html. The archives can be found at http://gort.ucsd.edu/newjour/.
12. To subscribe to the *Newsletter on Serials Pricing Issues*, send a message to listproc@unc.edu that reads: SUBSCRIBE PRICES Firstname Lastname.
13. Jeri Van Goethem, "Automated Acquisitions/In-Process Control Discussion Group: Using Technology's Tools: Introduction," *Library Acquisitions: Practice & Theory* 19, no.3 (Fall 1995): 357-358.
14. A general discussion can be found in Tona Henderson, "Weaving the Web: Using the World Wide Web in Library Acquisitions," *Library Acquisitions: Practice & Theory* 20, no. 3 (Fall 1996): 367-374.
15. See also: Barbara Stewart. *Neal-Schuman Directory of Library Technical Services Home Pages* (New York: Neal-Schuman, 1997).

16. To subscribe to LIBLICENSE-L, complete the online form at http://www.library.yale.edu/~llicense/mailing-list.shtml. The archives can be found at http://www.library.yale.edu/~llicense/ListArchives/.

17. See also: Steve Johnson, "Library Acquisitions Pages on the World Wide Web," *Library Acquisitions: Practice & Theory* 21, no. 2 (Summer 1997): 195-204.

18. "BNA PLUS," The Bureau of National Affairs, Inc. home page, 1997. http://www.bna.com/bnaplus/index.html (3 April 1998).

19. Rob Richards, "The Shape of Legal Publishing Today," University of Colorado Technical Services Home Page, 1998. http://www.colorado.edu/law/lawlib/ts/descr.htm (4 April 1998).

20. "GobiLink: Integrating GOBI and Your Library System," Yankee Book Peddler, Inc. home page, 1997. http://www.ybp.com/gobilink.htm (3 April 1998).

21. Viriginia M. Scheschy, "Technical Services and the World Wide Web," Untangling the Web home page, 1996. http://www.library.ucsb.edu/untangle/scheschy.html (3 April 1998).

Human Factors in the Electronic Technical Services

Joni Gomez

SUMMARY. This article explores the human resources implications due to technological changes in libraries, particularly the proliferation of internet resources and electronic journals. Skills required by library personnel have increased with the proliferation of serial titles and formats. Use of multiple systems to perform routine functions requires greater understanding of the interrelatedness of library units and connectivity of technology. Shifts in workloads and workflow, requiring staff with different skill levels and backgrounds, have resulted in reallocation of human resources in libraries. Training in several areas–aspects of librarianship, technology, and interpersonal skills–must be ongoing. Human reactions to technological change will determine the success or failure of technology. Training and communication are the keys to managing change, alleviating anxiety in the workplace, and success. *[Article copies available for a fee from The Haworth Document Delivery Service: 1-800-342-9678. E-mail address: getinfo@haworthpressinc.com]*

INTRODUCTION

Library literature is replete with articles on the implementation of technology, programs and services. The pace and pervasiveness of technological change has touched every aspect of the work we do in libraries. While the nature of librarianship is still the traditional selection, acquisition, organiza-

---

Joni Gomez is Technical Services Law Librarian at University of Oregon Law Library, Eugene, OR 97403-1221.

[Haworth co-indexing entry note]: "Human Factors in the Electronic Technical Services." Gomez, Joni. Co-published simultaneously in *The Acquisitions Librarian* (The Haworth Press, Inc.) No. 21, 1999, pp. 105-114; and: *Periodical Acquisitions and the Internet* (ed: Nancy Slight-Gibney) The Haworth Press, Inc., 1999, pp. 105-114. Single or multiple copies of this article are available for a fee from The Haworth Document Delivery Service [1-800-342-9678, 9:00 a.m. - 5:00 p.m. (EST). E-mail address: getinfo@haworthpressinc.com].

© 1999 by The Haworth Press, Inc. All rights reserved.

tion and facilitation of access to information, the "what" and "how" are in flux; the constant in the equation is the "who." The "who" includes many diverse players, including patrons who have information needs, researchers and writers who create the information, publishers who package the information, vendors who market and provide enhanced access to the information. But most importantly, the "who" includes library staff who bridge the gap between the patron and the information.

Any success of new technology, new programs and services must be attributed in part to the hard work of innovative and dedicated staff; every failure harkens back to a failure to address the human needs–failure to involve staff in the planning process, failure to communicate, failure to train, failure to set common goals and work together to achieve them.

And while the human element remains a constant in providing library services, people themselves are continuously required to change and adapt to new equipment, new software, new procedures, new workflow, new work assignments, new work relationships. Each technological advancement affects people in the library. The impact of technology on library staff raises several human resource issues. The ways in which libraries are dealing with these issues are as many and varied as the libraries themselves.

IMPACT OF TECHNOLOGY ON STAFF

In early studies of human factors in factory automation, Ann Majchrzak identified six parameters as having important and independent effects on human resources: integration, rigidity, reliability, workflow unpredictability, feedback, and safety.[1] These same elements can be considered in examining the impact on library staff resulting from the proliferation of electronic publications and increased internet access.

Integration

Majchrzak defines integration in terms of organizational structure. "Every organization, in order to maintain control, must divide its staff, functions and process into distinguishable units. This is called differentiation. Yet it is also necessary for these people, functions, and processes to be closely coordinated. This is called integration."[2]

With the advent of integrated library systems we have already experienced a merging and shifting of traditional technical service functions. For example, shared bibliographic records necessitated the coordination of the work of acquisitions staff and catalogers. The need for greater standardization and accommodation of system requirements made apparent the need for greater communication and cooperation between library units. Job analysis and workflow studies revealed duplicate efforts and outdated tasks resulting in changes in procedures to streamline and eliminate redundancy.

The explosion of electronic journals and internet resources has contributed to the further breakdown of traditional functional lines of library organization. Selection of serials titles now includes decisions on content, format, pricing policy, and weighing complex alternatives. Electronic publications may not be the exact equivalent of their print counterparts. Articles may be excluded if the author retained copyright. Other material such as letters-to-the-editor may be excluded as well. The variety of formats–paper, digital, audiovisual, microfilm, full text or only table of contents–requires careful consideration and a knowledge of user needs due to the fact that decisions as to format will impact how it is accessed and disseminated. Understanding hardware, software and other system requirements such as wiring and connectivity for internet access are imperative and format choice may require coordination with systems experts. Fee structures have many negotiable options including subscriptions per title, per article, per use, connect time, and print charges. Licensing agreements may take into account patron base, consortiums and groups of institutions such as state systems that include multiple institutions, campuses or branches. It often takes a team of subject experts, collection development and acquisitions librarians, and systems staff to make purchasing decisions.

Shared responsibility and coordination of library functions goes beyond traditional technical service units when dealing with electronic publications. Preservation decisions as to whether to archive locally and in which format will affect access, as will the decision as to whether and how to represent internet titles in the online catalog. Notes in the bibliographic and holdings records reflecting format and electronic location will affect user access and the degree of public service assistance required. Maintaining records in the online catalog for internet publications not locally archived requires ongoing maintenance to check URL addresses and other links to ensure continued access.

Libraries can no longer delineate clear areas of bibliographic responsibility with shared records and multiple uses. Library administrators and managers are faced with the staffing dilemma of who will take on these additional responsibilities and tasks. Public service staff will need to understand changes in cataloging rules and MARC codes to facilitate access and instruct users. Accessing a journal title is no longer just a question of physical location, but now includes equipment and software. In addition, public service staff will need to educate users on features unique to electronic titles including "dynamic" articles or papers which are updated with "comments" files, full-text searching, audiovisual and hypertext links. Catalogers will have to make decisions in consultation with collection development and public service librarians based on user needs when constructing bibliographic records.

Coordination of services may extend beyond the library to include campus computing centers. For acquisitions librarians, integration extends to campus fiscal departments as well as publishers, vendors, and bibliographic utilities who conduct business on the internet. For collection development librarians, integration extends to campus legal departments for assistance in crafting licensing agreements and aid in interpreting contracts. Collection development librarians also work with their colleagues in consortia to coordinate access and cost-sharing benefits.

Rigidity

The degree of rigidity of the new technology, another parameter identified by Majchrzak, affects job tasks and priorities. A high level of skill and flexibility is needed to process non-traditional materials. Staff working on the internet need to learn e-mail to communicate with vendors or subscribe to lists, file transfer protocol (FTP), gopher, Telnet, and World Wide Web. Staff also need an understanding of the structure of the new formats in order to process them. Electronic journals may be published in complete issues or released article by article as each is ready. Electronic resources require different processing by check-in staff since they may be received differently, archived differently, and thus require different information recorded about them for both bibliographic and holdings records. Many libraries opt not to create check-in records for electronic resources not physically acquired and locally archived by the library. This lack of opportunity to examine each issue creates additional maintenance issues such as how to deal with title changes.[3] The acquisition of electronic journals may be characterized as an extreme lack of rigidity. Providing bibliographic access to such fluid entities requires overcoming some of the rigidity inherent in existing bibliographic format rules.

Reliability

Reliability of new technology has a tremendous impact on staff in the library. Every aspect of serials work in the library today requires the use of a computer. Selecting, ordering, invoicing, receiving, payment, cataloging, check-in, claims, searching and document delivery all require access to any number of systems. It is essential to keep equipment and systems functioning to perform the day-to-day tasks. This necessitates increased need for diagnostics skills and technical knowledge to trouble-shoot hardware and software, as well as increased knowledge about information system design to enable adequate communication regarding problems or needs to systems staff and programmers.

Workflow Unpredictability

Fluctuations in work load are a standard feature of acquisitions departments as they cope with publishing cycles, budget cycles and in some cases academic calendars. However, much of this fluctuation is predictable. Workflow unpredictability can also stem from a number of sources. Equipment failures, delays in delivery of materials and supplies, and staff absenteeism are examples of problems that can interrupt workflow. For technology to be successful there must be a human infrastructure that promotes sufficient knowledge and abilities, flexibility, decision-making, and responsibility to cope with unpredictable change.

Feedback

Feedback has an impact on humans in the workplace. Work in a serials department prior to automation was quite isolated. Staff assigned to serial check-in, for example, could sort mail, note receipt in the Kardex files and facilitate processing and shelving without significant interaction with other library units. Automated check-in resulted in the need for communication and coordination with catalogers so that holdings information would be maintained following system and cataloging standards. Work being performed on the internet has widened the circle of contact to public service staff who must interpret records and to systems staff who maintain equipment and software. Decisions made on how to handle check-in of electronic journals and internet resources impact every library unit as well as the users of the online catalog. It is imperative that check-in staff receive timely feedback on work performed so mistakes can be corrected or procedures changed to make the information in the catalog readily apparent to the users.

Safety

Safety is the final parameter identified by Majchrzak as having an important effect on human resources. As library tasks shifted from manual to automated, staff jobs became increasingly sedentary with long hours in front of a computer terminal. Internet access has only added to the amount of time spent in front of a terminal. Libraries have faced a growing number of staff affected by repetitive motion injuries such as carpal tunnel syndrome and eye strain from jobs that are dependent upon computers. Ergonomic work stations and task analysis can help ameliorate some of their problems.

TRAINING NEEDS

The more integrated the system, the larger the training needs. Since the work of each library unit impacts that of all others, staff today are expected to understand the larger picture. With a shared online catalog, all staff must understand the structure of the online catalog and the information contained within, whether they are inputting the data for placing orders or interpreting a bibliographic or holdings record for a patron. This necessitates the need for ongoing and continuous training on the many system components.

For academic acquisitions librarians and staff, knowledge of the online catalog is just one piece of the complex puzzle which now also includes knowledge of the systems used by publishers and vendors, knowledge of the fiscal system of the parent institution, and knowledge of campus resources to facilitate internet access.

Systems training is accomplished in many ways: informally on-the-job or formally through courses, through workshops and seminars. With the implementation of new systems, consultants may be brought in to train library staff. Commercial partners may offer many options. For example, OCLC provides regular workshops, user group meetings, and often sends representatives to library conferences to provide training opportunities nationwide and locally for library staff.

Many large libraries have created staff positions to meet system training demands. Centralized training provides a thorough and consistent introduction for newly hired staff and ensures library-wide training when hardware and software upgrades occur. More often, training positions serve in a coordinator function, such as the University of Oregon's Information Technology Center Program Coordinator, who works with librarians and library staff, campus computing staff, and other faculty to provide an array of workshops and services offered free of charge to all staff and students. These workshops, which include an introduction to the internet for beginners and advanced courses on web searching, web page design and html editing, have proven enormously popular with library staff based on enrollment and evaluations from participants.

Further, integration of functions results in additional training needs for library staff. Because library units are interconnected due to the shared technology, interpersonal skills are essential in building working relationships, and in coordinating work between units. Acquisitions librarians need these same skills for building external partnerships and when negotiating with publishers and vendors. Often campus resources can be called upon to provide training for library staff. Campus human resources departments often offer supervisory training and special needs workshops such as customer service, conflict management, and first aid.

In addition, in order to keep systems and equipment operational, all must have the rudimentary skills for troubleshooting hardware and software, or must know who to call and be able to communicate problems effectively. Often staff are called upon to evaluate and make selections for hardware purchases, telecommunications access, internet and network connections, software, CD-ROM storage and preservation for managing electronic resources.

The skills and knowledge required to perform the work of serials management has increased dramatically with the advent of internet access and new technology. Not only have we seen a proliferation of titles and formats, acquisition librarians must contend with more publishers and more vendors, each with their own system. Expectations of knowledge required to manage serials in today's workplace include cost accounting, marketing, strategic planning, negotiation, product development, research and analysis, and management information systems.[4]

HUMAN RESOURCE ISSUES

In addition to training, the impact of technology on library staff has raised a number of other human resource issues including compensation, job classification, staffing levels, reallocation of staff, and team building. The increased number of titles and formats has led to higher expectations of performance, the requirement of a wider range of knowledge and skills, and greater responsibility and decision-making placed on staff. Questions of compensation have led libraries to look at existing classifications systems, job descriptions and job specifications.

The use of technology has led to a broadening of job classifications and blurring of distinctions between classification levels within libraries. Technology has resulted in a shift of responsibility and decision-making further down classification levels. For example, serials check-in has always been high volume work, performed by staff at lower classification levels. Prior to automation, skills required were the ability to read, and to mark the appropriate Kardex to indicate receipt. With the automated catalog, skills required were increased to basic computer literacy and keyboarding ability. Today, serials check-in staff are required to have advanced computer skills and be able to navigate on the internet. Further, they must be able to recognize non-print titles, understand the complex licensing and copyright restrictions associated with each and be savvy enough to pass on the appropriate information to other units within the library, work previously performed at higher job classifications.[5]

Automated systems have facilitated routine tasks in library acquisitions, reducing the need for work previously performed by staff at the lower job classification levels. At the same time, automated systems have resulted in the need for staff to perform many new duties including planning, coordinating, performing research and analysis and preparing management reports which have typically been done by staff in higher classifications. The emphasis on technology has resulted in the need for staff with different types of abilities. Newly-created positions often require skills in the area of computer science or information science rather than library science. The shift in focus from ownership to access requires a commitment of additional staff to meet interlibrary loan and document delivery demands. In addition, the internet has presented librarians with expanded roles in scholarly communication, the protection of intellectual and property rights and privacy issues.

Integration has further affected staffing considerations as staff with interpersonal and communication skills are sought to fill positions that primarily deal with coordination and training. The success of library programs and services is dependent on staff working together to accomplish common goals. There is a recognized need for team building and group problem solving skills.

WAYS LIBRARIES ARE RESPONDING TO HUMAN RESOURCE ISSUES

Budgetary restrictions have impacted the way libraries have responded to human resource issues. Funding is not available to add additional staff to perform new duties created by new technology and alternate publication formats. Libraries have redefined goals, prioritized functions and reallocated human resources accordingly. When vacant, each position is reassessed. Job duties and skills requirements are updated. When reassignments are made with existing staff, efforts are made whenever possible to match individual skills and interests with library needs.

Libraries have seen a flattening of organization as a result of integration and have responded with a number of approaches. Several have undergone reorganization to formally create new less-rigid working relationships. Others have adopted Total Quality Management (TQM) and attempted to increase staff involvement on committees and task forces.

Job classifications are being rewritten to reflect the impact of technology. The trend has been to focus on job roles rather than individual tasks. Likewise, performance evaluations more often reflect team efforts and unit missions rather than individual accomplishments and focus on flexibility, goals, standards, and staff development.

Safety concerns are a priority for libraries. Many libraries have training programs that include accident prevention. Ergonomic considerations are taken into account in designing work areas and determining workflows, purchasing furniture and equipment and providing proper illumination to eliminate screen glare. Staff are provided with adjustable seats, foot and wrist rests, and document holders in an attempt to alleviate potential injuries.

COMMUNICATION AND TRAINING AS A MEANS OF DEALING WITH ANXIETY IN THE WORKPLACE

The results of working in a rapidly changing and demanding environment where staff are required to be more flexible, have more knowledge, to have a greater diversity of skills, to process an increasing number of titles in wider formats, and to interact with other staff at a wider range of organizational levels have led to increased anxiety in the workplace. Staff may become overwhelmed by the amount of technical information and related responsibilities, intimidated by learning new skills, or lack confidence when co-workers seem better prepared to handle the new technology. Many libraries have found communication to be the key to alleviating stress. Communication can be as simple as publishing a newsletter or holding open meetings and inviting staff input. Team building takes place formally through widespread participation on committees and informally with participation in staff associations, talent shows, sports and social events.

The internet has added several layers to the already complex world of library automation. By looking at the ways technology has impacted human resources using Majchrzak's six parameters: integration, rigidity, reliability, workflow unpredictability, feedback, and safety, libraries can work towards improving the workplace and facilitating change in such a way that people can adapt and feel comfortable. The key elements are communication and training. Success today requires a commitment to continuous education and staff development. While technology is an important component in library service, without the commitment and dedication of people there can be no success.

REFERENCES

1. Ann Majchrzak, *The Human Side of Factory Automation*. San Francisco: Jossey-Bass Publishers, 1988.
2. Majchrzak, *Human Side*, p. 225.
3. Betty Landesman, "Keeping the Jell-O® Nailed to the Wall: Maintaining and Managing the Virtual Collection," *The Serials Librarian* 30(3/4): 137-147.
4. Esther Green Bierbaum, "Plugged-In Jell-O™: Taught or Caught?" *The Serials Librarian* 29(3/4): 89-103.
5. Nancy L. Buchanan, "Navigating the Electronic River: Electronic Product Licensing and Contracts," *The Serials Librarian* 30(3/4): 171-182.

BIBLIOGRAPHY

Brooke, F. Dixon, Jr., "Subscription of Information Agency Services in the Electronic Era," *The Serials Librarian* 29(3/4): 57-65.

Clark, Katie and Sally Kalin, "Technostressed Out? How to Cope in the Digital Age," *Library Journal* 121(13): 30-32.

Cooley, Elizabeth (Libby) and Edward A. Goedeken, "The Significance of Information Provision and Content: Libraries as Information Providers Instead of Format Collectors," *The Serials Librarian* 29(3/4): 47-56.

Gozzi, Cynthia, "Managing Acquisitions in a Changing Environment: From Coping to Comfort," *Library Resources & Technical Services* 41(2): 136-138.

Horny, Karen L., "Fifteen Years of Automation: Evolution of Technical Services Staffing," *Library Resources & Technical Services* 31(1): 69-76.

Oskamp, Stuart and Shirlynn Spacapan (Ed.), *People's Reactions to Technology*. Newbury Park, CA: Sage Publications, 1990.

Ungern-Sternberg, Sara von and Mats G. Lindquist, "The Impact of Electronic Journals on Library Functions," *Journal of Information Science*, 21(5): 396-401.

Index

Abstracting and indexing services, online, 84-85. *See also* Indexes, electronic
Access, to electronic publications, 29-33,77,79
  added, 27
  cost of, 24-25,26,38-41
  free, 24,48,62
  hidden and indirect, 26
  Internet Protocol address use in, 30-31
  ownership versus, 7,9,41,59
  by password, 31
  perpetual, 29,34,41
  promotional offers for, 9
  remote, 9,29-31
  to second-generation electronic journals, 14
  testing of availability of, 14-15,16
  time length of, 9
  timeliness of, 28
  on trial basis, 47-48
  usage statistics for, 18,28-29
  by users, 15,16,17-18
AACR2, 79
ACQNET, 95
Acquisition, of electronic products, 5-19
  complexity of, 1,5
  decision-making in, 3,5-19
Acquisition staff, responsibilities of, 37-38
AcqWeb, 96
Adobe Acrobat, 31,32
Aggregator services, 2,7
  electronic indexes provided by, 27
  number of full-text journals provided by, 22-23
  perpetual access provided by, 34

American Association for the Advancement of Science, 48
American Association of Law Libraries, 95
American Bar Association, 98
American Institute of Physics, 44
American Libraries, 37
American University, Washington College of Law Library, Internet use by, 93-103
  e-mail, 94-95,96
  file transfer protocol, 95-96
  INNOPAC and, 94,95,96,101
  law libraries' home pages, 97
  listservs, 95
  publishers' web sites, 97-100
  vendors' web sites, 100-101
  World Wide Web, 96-97
Andrews, W.L., 48
Anglo-American Cataloging Rules 2, 79
Aninao, Cynthia, 95
Annual Survey of Child Nutrition, 52-53
ANSI/NISO Z39.56 standard, 84
Archiving, of electronic publications, 10,28,29,33-35,60
  by consortia, 2,59-60
  technical aspects of, 33,34
  University of Arizona policy for, 59-60
ARC Statistics, 38
ARL Newsletter, 60
ARL Supplementary Statistics Questionnaire, 38-39
Articles, in journals
  hypertext links to, 32
  locating of, 27
ASCII, 6-7

Association for Library Collections and Technical Services, Collection Management and Development Section, Chief Collection Development Officers of Large Research Libraries Discussion Group, Budget Survey by, 39,41
Association of American Publishers, 86,88
Association of Research Libraries (ARL), 22,38
  Licensing Electronic Information web site, 60-61
  member libraries' electronic journal use, 22
Authenticity, of electronic-based information, 59

Bancroft-Whitney, 99-100
Barcodes, 85
Bibliographic instruction, 17-18
Bibliographic records, of electronic publications, 79,108
  web addresses in, 15
Bibliographies, hypertext links to, 32
Blackwell
  Electronic Journal Navigator, 10,22-23
  Information Services, 100
Bookman, The, 48
Bowker, R.R., 86
Budgets
  electronic resource allocations of, 38-41,49
  effect on human resources issues, 112
Bundling, of electronic journal titles, 25,83-84
Bureau of National Affairs, 98
Butterworth Legal Publishing, 99

Campus computing centers, 108,110
Canada, Electronic Publications, Pilot program, 73,75

Carpal tunnel syndrome, 109
Catalogers, collaborative approach of, 107-108
Cataloging, of electronic publications, 27,33,77-78,79-80
  staff's knowledge of, 110
Catalogs, online. *See also* Bibliographic records
  electronic journal access, 15
  hypertext links, 33,77-78,79-80
  of law libraries, Web access, 97
Catchword, 31
CD-ROM
  annual cumulations on, 29
  conversion to, 75
  cost of, 52
  electronic journals on, 7
  ownership of, 9
Census of Population (1960), 59
Check-in procedures, 14,108,109,111
Citation databases, 8
Citations, locating of, 27
Clark Boardman Callaghan, 99-100
Code Structure Identifiers, 85
Collection development, 23-24,26, 76-78
Collection development groups, 61
Comma-delimited text, 75
Commerce Business Daily, 52
Commerce Clearing House, Inc., 98-99
Committee on Institutional Cooperation, 42,59-60
  Electronic Journal Collection, 34
Communication
  as response to technological change, 113
  scholarly, impact of electronic publishing on, 3
Congressional Record, 73
Congressional Universe, 94
CONNECT, 100
Consortia
  electronic journal archiving by, 2,34,59-60

electronic journal subscriptions of, 25,83-84
Consumer Price Index Detailed Report, 52
Conversion, to electronic formats, 74-76
Copyright, 3,26,60,84,86
Cornell University, Mann Library, 61
Corporation for National Research Initiatives, 86
  HANDLE System, 88
Currency converter, 101
Current Index to Legal Periodicals (CILP), 96
Customization, of electronic journals, 28,96

Decision-making, in acquisitions, 3, 5-19
Depository libraries, 58-59,61,72,77, 78. *See also* University of Arizona
  new initiatives by, 61-62
  subscription fees for, 53
Depository Library Act, 62
Digital libraries, 63
Digital Object Identifier (DOI), 86-87, 88-89
Disabled users, 22,28
Diskettes
  electronic journals on, 7
  ownership of, 9
Document delivery services, 63,84-85
Downloaded copies, ownership of, 9
Dragon Dictate, 28
Duplicate copies, 58

Earned Degrees Conferred in the U.S., 52-53
EDGAR, 53
Education in Canada, 74
Electronic Data Interchange (EDI), 2, 85

Electronic journals. *See also* specific titles of journals
  availability of, 6,16-17
  delivery of, 6
  downloading of, 32-33
  first-generation, 6,14
  incompleteness and unreliability of, 58-69
  lack of standardization of, 5
  partial issues of, 58
  prevalence of use of, 22
  print journals versus, 24-25,27,52, 58,59
  second-generation, 6,14
  subscription-based, 6,7
  technical support for, 9,10-11,53
  as text files, 32
  usage statistics for, 18,28-29
Electronic publications. *See also* Electronic journals; specific titles
  access to. *See* Access, to electronic publications
  cost of, 52
  multiple formats of, 77
  print publications versus, 52
  technical support for, 53
e-mail, 94-95
  as electronic journal delivery method, 6-7,14
  use in electronic journal ordering, 13
  staff's familiarity with, 108
Encyclopedia Britannica Online, 63
Ergonomics, 109,112-113
ERIC, 62
European Union, 73
Expanded Academic Index, 58
Eye strain, computer use-related, 109, 112-113

Fair use, 60. *See also* Copyright
Fax, use in electronic journal ordering, 13

Federal Depository Library Program, 62,73,77. *See also* Depository libraries
Federal Express, 101
Federal Information Access Act of 1997, 62
Federal Register, 52
Fee structures, of electronic journals, 107
File transfer protocol (FTP), 95-96,108
Folmsbee, Mark, 95
Footnotes, hyperlinks to, 27
Formats, of electronic publications, 31
  multiple, 44
  portable document (PDF), 31,32
  proprietary, 31-32
Frankfurt Book Fair, 86-87

Gates, Bill, 43
Gateway systems, 63
Geographic Information System, 61
Georgetown University, E.B. Williams Law Library, 94,97
George Washington University Law Library, 94
Ghostscript, 32
Ghostview, 32
GOBI, 101
GOVDOC-L, 62
Government documents/serials
  electronic, 71-81
    archiving of, 59
    bibliographic control of, 72
    discontinuations of, 72
    formal conversion forms for, 75-76
    free access to, 62
    as "fugitive" publications, 78
    initiatives related to, 61-63
    lack of reliability of, 58-59
    privatization of, 52-53
    publishing costs, 52-53
  on microfiche, 72
  title variations of, 72

Government document services, organizational structure of, 61
Government Printing Office, 52,62,72
Guide to Selecting and Acquiring CD-ROMs, Software, and Other Electronic Publications, 56

Hale, Marylou, 93-94
Hardware
  future developments in, 53
  staff's responsibility for, 108-109, 110-111
Health aspects, of electronic technology, 109,112-113
HEIN-SUBS-L, 95
HTML (hypertext markup language), 32,75
Human resource implications, of technological changes, 105-114
  feedback, 109
  integration, 106-108,112
  job classification, 111-112
  libraries' responses to, 112-113
  reliability, 108-109
  rigidity, 108
  safety and health effects, 109, 112-113
  training needs related to, 110-111, 113
  workflow unpredictability, 109
Hyperlinks, as cataloging adjunct, 33, 77-78,79-80
Hypertext markup language (HTML), 32,75

IAC, Remote Patron Authentication Service (RPAS) of, 30
Independent, 48
Indexes, electronic, 27,28,53
Information Superhighway, 37
Inlarge, 28

INNOPAC, 94,95,96,101
Innovative Interface, Inc., 30
Institute of Physics, 28
"Intangible electronic documents," as library collection component, 63-64
Interlibrary loan, 18
Internal Digital Object Identifier Foundation, 87
International Standard Book Number, (ISBN), 87
International Standard Serial Number (ISSN), 85,87
Internet. *See also* Electronic journals; Electronic publications; World Wide Web
　serial items identification standards for. *See* Unique item identifiers
　staff's familiarity with, 108
Internet Grateful Med, 62
Internet Protocol (IP) number, 14, 15,30
Internet Service Provider (ISP), 30
Invoice processing, with file transfer protocol, 96
Iowa State University, 42

JAWS, 28
Job classification, impact of electronic technology on, 111-112
Johns Hopkins University Press, 32,44
Journal of Political Ecology, 60
Journal of the National Cancer Institute, 53
Jumpstations, 22

Kerberos, 30-31

LAWACQ, 95
LAW-LIB listserv, 95,100
Law libraries, Internet use by, 93-103
　e-mail, 94-95,96

file transfer protocol, 95-96
INNOPAC and, 94,95,96,101
law libraries' home pages, 97
listservs, 95
publishers' web sites, 97-100
vendors' web sites, 100-101
World Wide Web, 96-97
Lawyers Cooperative Publishing, 99-100
Legal issues, in electronic journal acquisition, 8,9-10. *See also* Copyright; Licensing agreements
Legal Publishers List: The Shape of Legal Publishing Today, 100
Legal Resource Index, 94
Legislation, electronically-formatted, 52
Leiserson, Anna Belle, 96
Lexis Law Publishing, 99
LIBLICENSE: Licensing Digital Information, 10,60,96-97
Libraries. *See also* Depository libraries; names of specific libraries
　electronic information-related trends in, 63
Licensing agreements, 2,9-10,15, 25-26,38,107
　information sources for, 3,60-61, 96-97
　negotiations for, 9-10,43
　University of Arizona policy for, 60-61
Licensing Electronic Information, 60-61
Listservs, 95
Local area networks (LANs), 42,43
Lynch, Clifford, 1

MARC, 79
Matthew Bender Site, 99
MEDLINE, 62
Metasites, 22
Michie Company, 99
Microfiche conversion project, 72
Montgomery, Jack, 94

National Archives and Records
    Administration, 59
National Commission on Libraries and
    Information Science, 62
National Information Standards
    Organization (NISO), 84
National Library of Medicine, 62
National Technical Information
    Service (NTIS), 53,62
NEWJOUR, 95
NEWLAWBOOKS-L, 95
Newsletter on Serials Pricing Issues,
    95
*New York Magazine; or Literary
    Repository*, 48
NOTIS system, 41-42,43,45

OCLC
    electronic journal archiving by, 29
    ERIC reports and, 62
    FirstSearch Electronic Collections
        Online, 10,22-23,34
    Persistent Uniform Resource
        Locator (PURL) system, 88
    systems training by, 110
Okerson, Ann, 41
O'Donnell, James J., 95
Ordering
    communication modalities for, 13
    complications of, 10-12
    information required for, 8-10,14
    online, 12-13
Outspoken, 28
Overseas Business Reports (U.S. Dept.
    of Commerce), 76
Oxford University Press, 553

Package deals, in electronic journal
    subscriptions, 25,83-84
Packages, tracking of, 101
Paper-based publications. *See* Print
    (paper-based) publications
Passwords
    for electronic journal access, 31

for vendor/publisher online orders,
    13,14,17
PDF (portable document format), 31,
    32
Persistent Uniform Resource Locator
    (PURL) system, 88
*Policy for Acquiring and Selecting
    Electronic Products*
    (University of Arizona)
    development of, 55-57
    issues addressed by, 58-61
        archiving, 59-60
        copyright, 60
        duplicate copies, 58
        incompleteness and unreliability
            of products, 58-59
        licensing and leasing, 60-61
Portable document format (PDF),
    31,32
Postscript files, 28,31,32
Preservation. *See also* Archiving
    of electronic journals, 29,107
Pricing models, for electronic journals,
    24-26
Print (paper-based) publications
    cost of, 52
    electronic publication access
        provided with, 24
    electronic publications versus,
        24-25,27,52,58,59
    limited user availability of, 27
    printouts of, ownership of, 9
    usage studies of, 28-29
Project Muse, 29,32,44,45-46
Public service staff, 17,107
Publisher Item Identifier (PII),
    86,87,88,89
Publishers. *See also* specific
    publishers
    electronic journal services of, 7,8
    legal, Web sites of, 97-100
    licensing agreements with. *See*
        Licensing agreements
    online systems of, 12-13
    scientific, technical, and medical,
        87

societal, journal archive access by, 29

R.R. Bowker, 86
Readers, for visually-impaired users, 22,28
RealPage, 31
Reed Elsevier, Inc., 86
Remote access, 9,29-31
Remote Patron Authentication Service (RPAS), 30
Repetitive motion injuries, 109
Research Institute of America, 99
Richards, Rob, 100
Rich Text Format, 31

Safety aspects, of electronic technology, 109,112-113
Science, 47
Securities and Exchange Committee, 53
Selection criteria, for electronic journals, 26-29,107
SERIALIST, 95
Serial Item and Contribution Identifier (SICI), 84-86,88-89
Serials Industry Systems Advisory Committee, 88
Serials in Microform, 101
Shepard's Citations, 99
Software, 53
  staff's responsibility for, 108-109, 110-111
Southwest Institute for Research on Women, 60
Southwest Jewish History, 60
Staff. *See also* Acquisitions staff; Public services staff
  impact of electronic technical services on, 105-114
  job classification issues, 111-112
  training issues, 3,110-111,113
Statistics

budgetary, 38-42
of electronic journal usage, 18,28-29
Statistics Canada, 73,74
STAT-USA, 53,77
Stevens, Peter, 97
Stewart, Barbara, 96
Storage requirements, for electronic journals, 28
Study to Identify Measures Necessary for a Succcessful Transition to a More Electronic Federal Depository Library Program, 73
Subscription agents, electronic publications services of, 2, 7-8,10-11
  for legal materials, 97
SwetsNet, 22-233

Tab-delimited text, 75
"Tangible objects," as library collection component, 63-64
Technical Processing Online Tools, 96
Technical Services Law Librarian, 95
Technical skills, training in, 3, 110-111,113
Technological change, human resources implications of, 105-141. *See* Human resource implications, of technological changes
Telnet, 108
THOMAS, 94
3M Innovation, 37
Top 200 Technical Services Benefits of Home Page Development, 96
Total quality management, 112
Training
  for electronic journal use, 17-18
  in technical skills, 3,110-111,113
Trial subscriptions, 47-48

UMI, 101

Uniform Resource Locators (URLs),
    87-88,107
  dependability of, 58-59
  use with Internet Protocol
    addresses, 30
  stability of, 29
  of vendors and publishers, 96
Uniform Resource Names (URNs),
    87-88
Unique item identifiers, 83-91
  Digital Object Identifier (DOI),
    86-87,88-89
  Publisher Item Identifier (PII), 86,
    87,88,89
  Serial Item and Contribution
    Identifier (SICI), 84-86,
    88-89
  Uniform Resource Locators
    (URLs), 29,30,58-59,
    87-88,107
  Uniform Resource Name (URN),
    87-88
United Parcel Service, 101
U. S. Department of Commerce, 53
U. S. Government Printing Office, 52,
    62,72
U. S. Superintendent of Documents,
    78
University of Arizona
  collection development groups, 61
  consortial arrangements of, 63
  *Policy for Acquiring and Selecting
    Electronic Products,* 51-69
University of California, Davis, access
    to NTIS electronic image
    files, 62
University of Cincinnati Law Library,
    95
University of Colorado Law Library,
    Technical Services Home
    Page, 97
University of Colorado Law School,
    100
University of Iowa Libraries
  acquisitions practices, 41-48

  electronic materials subscription
    costs, 39,40
  NOTIS system, 41-42,43,45
University of Nevada, Las Vegas,
    93-94
University of Oregon Library System
  electronic journal cataloging
    practices, 27
  electronic journal collection
    development policy, 23,24
  Information Technology Center
    Program Coordinate, 110
University of Virginia Law Library, 97
University of Washington Libraries
  Acquisitions Division, 97
  Law Library, 96
Usage studies, statistics for, 18,28-29
Users
  acceptance of electronic journals
    by, 19
  authorized, 29-31
  awareness of electronic journals,
    29,33
  disabled, 22,28
  electronic journal access by, 15,16,
    17-18
    remote, 29-31
  expectations of, 52
  number of, 27

Vanderbilt University Law Library, 96
Vendors
  of legal materials, 100
  negotiations with, 3
  online systems of, 12-13
  overseas, e-mail communication
    with, 94
  web sites, 100-101
Verification process, in electronic
    journal acquisition, 8-10,13
Virtual library, 63
Visually-impaired users, 22,28

Warren, Gorham & Lamont, 99

Washburn University Law Library, 95
Web Access Management, 30
Web browsers, 32-33
    Digital Object Identifier directory searching with, 86
Web pages
    electronic journal titles on, 33
    hyperlinks to, 77-78,79-80
West Group, 99-100
Westlaw, 99-100
West Publishing, 99-100
William S. Hein Co., Inc., 95,100
Workflow
    for electronic access, 48-49
    unpredictability of, 109
Work stations
    ergonomics of, 109

    public access, 78
World Wide Web, 96-97
    as electronic journal delivery method, 6-7
    staff's familiarity with, 108

Xenon Laboratories, 101

Yale University, Lillian Goldman Law Library, 97
Yankee Book Peddlar, 101
Young, Jay, 53

ZoomText, 28

Haworth DOCUMENT DELIVERY SERVICE

This valuable service provides a single-article order form for any article from a Haworth journal.

- *Time Saving:* No running around from library to library to find a specific article.
- *Cost Effective:* All costs are kept down to a minimum.
- *Fast Delivery:* Choose from several options, including same-day FAX.
- *No Copyright Hassles:* You will be supplied by the original publisher.
- *Easy Payment:* Choose from several easy payment methods.

Open Accounts Welcome for . . .
- Library Interlibrary Loan Departments
- Library Network/Consortia Wishing to Provide Single-Article Services
- Indexing/Abstracting Services with Single Article Provision Services
- Document Provision Brokers and Freelance Information Service Providers

---

MAIL or *FAX* THIS ENTIRE ORDER FORM TO:

Haworth Document Delivery Service
The Haworth Press, Inc.
10 Alice Street
Binghamton, NY 13904-1580

or FAX: 1-800-895-0582
or CALL: 1-800-429-6784
9am-5pm EST

PLEASE SEND ME PHOTOCOPIES OF THE FOLLOWING SINGLE ARTICLES:

1) Journal Title: _____
   Vol/Issue/Year: _____ Starting & Ending Pages: _____
   Article Title: _____

2) Journal Title: _____
   Vol/Issue/Year: _____ Starting & Ending Pages: _____
   Article Title: _____

3) Journal Title: _____
   Vol/Issue/Year: _____ Starting & Ending Pages: _____
   Article Title: _____

4) Journal Title: _____
   Vol/Issue/Year: _____ Starting & Ending Pages: _____
   Article Title: _____

(See other side for Costs and Payment Information)

COSTS: Please figure your cost to order quality copies of an article.
1. Set-up charge per article: $8.00
     ($8.00 × number of separate articles)   _____
2. Photocopying charge for each article:
     1-10 pages: $1.00   _____
     11-19 pages: $3.00   _____
     20-29 pages: $5.00   _____
     30+ pages: $2.00/10 pages   _____
3. Flexicover (optional): $2.00/article   _____
4. Postage & Handling: US: $1.00 for the first article/
     $.50 each additional article   _____
     Federal Express: $25.00   _____
     Outside US: $2.00 for first article/
     $.50 each additional article   _____
5. Same-day FAX service: $.50 per page   _____

GRAND TOTAL: _____

METHOD OF PAYMENT: (please check one)
❏ Check enclosed   ❏ Please ship and bill. PO # _____
     (sorry we can ship and bill to bookstores only! All others must pre-pay)
❏ Charge to my credit card: ❏ Visa;   ❏ MasterCard;   ❏ Discover;
                              ❏ American Express;

Account Number: _____   Expiration date: _____

Signature: X _____

Name: _____   Institution: _____

Address: _____

_____

City: _____   State: _____   Zip: _____

Phone Number: _____   FAX Number: _____

MAIL or *FAX* THIS ENTIRE ORDER FORM TO:

Haworth Document Delivery Service	**or FAX:** 1-800-895-0582
The Haworth Press, Inc.	**or CALL:** 1-800-429-6784
10 Alice Street	(9am-5pm EST)
Binghamton, NY 13904-1580	